EVERYTHING®

C·R·A·F·T·S

WEDDING
Decorations & Keepsakes

Add a Personal Touch to the Big Day!

Terry L. Rye and Jacquelynne Johnson

Adams Media

Avon, Massachusetts

An Everything® Series Book.
Everything® and everything.com® are registered trademarks of F+W Publications, Inc.

Published by Adams Media, an F+W Publications Company
57 Littlefield Street, Avon, MA 02322 U.S.A.
www.adamsmedia.com

ISBN: 1-59337-227-2
Printed in the United States of America.

J I H G F E D C B A

Library of Congress Cataloging-in-Publication Data
Rye, Terry L.
Everything crafts--wedding decorations & keepsakes / Terry L. Rye and Jacquelynne Johnson.
p.   cm.
(An everything series book)
ISBN 1-59337-227-2
1. Handicraft. 2. Wedding decorations. I. Title: Wedding decorations & keepsakes.
II. Johnson, Jacquelynne. III. Title. IV. Series: Everything series.

TT149.R72 2005
745.594'1--dc22

2004013571

This publication is designed to provide accurate and authoritative information with regard to the subject matter covered. It is sold with the understanding that the publisher is not engaged in rendering legal, accounting, or other professional advice. If legal advice or other expert assistance is required, the services of a competent professional person should be sought.

—From a *Declaration of Principles* jointly adopted by a Committee of the
American Bar Association and a Committee of Publishers and Associations

This book is available at quantity discounts for bulk purchases.
For information, call 1-800-872-5627.

Some material in this publication has been adapted and compiled from the following previously published works, listed by author:
Johnson, Jacquelynne   *Beautiful Bridal Accessories You Can Make* ©2002 (F+W Publications, Inc.)
Rye, Terry L.   *Creative Wedding Florals You Can Make* ©2000 (F+W Publications, Inc.)
Rye, Terry L. and Tudor, Laurel *Creative Wedding Keepsakes You Can Make* ©2000 (F+W Publications, Inc.)

Photographs by Christine Polomsky, Al Parrish, and Tim Grondin.

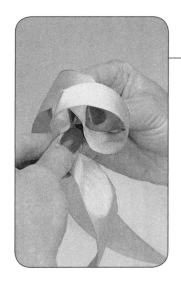

Part Three: Accessorize! • 65

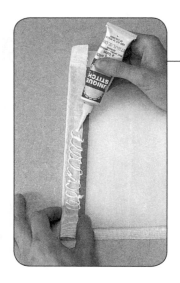

Part Four: Safe Keeping • 91

Welcome to the *Everything® Crafts* Series!

If you want to get in touch with your inner creativity but aren't sure where to begin, you've already completed Step One—choosing the perfect resource to help you get started. The EVERYTHING® CRAFTS books are ideal for beginners because they provide illustrated, step-by-step instruction for creating fun—and unique—projects.

The EVERYTHING® CRAFTS books bring the craft world back to the basics, providing easy-to-follow direction on finding appropriate tools and materials to learn new craft techniques. These clear and readable books guide you every step of the way, from beginning until end, teaching you tips and tricks to get your craft to look just right.

So sit back and enjoy. This experience is all about introducing you to the world of crafts—and, most of all, learning EVERYTHING you can!

A note to our readers:

The elegant decorations and keepsakes projects you find in *The Everything® Crafts Wedding Decoration & Keepsakes Book* are crafts that you can preserve and cherish for years to come. Without the talented contributors who spent much time and energy making sure anyone could duplicate these creative efforts at home, we would not be able to present this terrific collection of accessories, decorations, mementos, and florals. With that, we would like to offer many thanks to these contributors whose projects and amazing ideas further enhance what should be a remarkable and joyous occasion.

Special thanks goes to: Terry L. Rye, Jacquelynne Johnson, Laurel Tudor, Tricia Waddell, Greg Albert, Karen Roberts, Jolie Lamping Roth, Tim Grondin, Andrea Short, Jennifer Johnson, Julia Groh, everyone at Betterway Books, the Mariemont Florist, and Indian Hill Church. We hope that readers like you enjoy creating the special projects in this book.

—The Editors, the **EVERYTHING® CRAFTS** *Series*

Introduction

You probably think it's impossible to make the time to create something special—even if it's for your wedding day. It's easy to say you don't have the time—or the patience—to make a simple bouquet or hairpiece because there aren't enough hours in a day let alone enough hours to plan a wedding.

Weddings are one of life's oldest rituals, and the energy that goes into preparing for such a momentous occasion should reflect the personality and uniqueness of those involved. A long time ago, brides and their families and friends pitched in together to create wedding décor and props solely by hand.

The projects in this book are for those who don't necessarily create things by hand very often: They're for you, the beginner. They're for keeping costs low and beauty high, and they're for adding elegance to what will already be a day to remember for a lifetime.

Whether it's florals, keepsakes, or mementos you seek to create—have no fear, there's something for everyone. The rest is up to you.

Part One

The Basics

The Basics

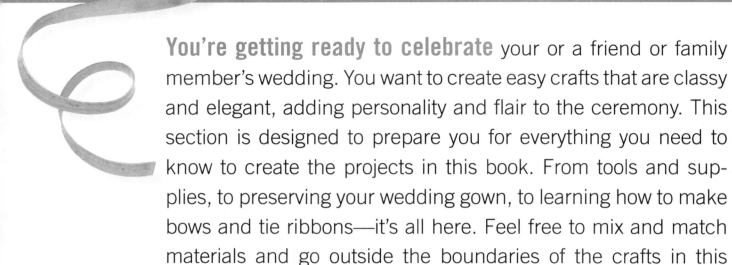

You're getting ready to celebrate your or a friend or family member's wedding. You want to create easy crafts that are classy and elegant, adding personality and flair to the ceremony. This section is designed to prepare you for everything you need to know to create the projects in this book. From tools and supplies, to preserving your wedding gown, to learning how to make bows and tie ribbons—it's all here. Feel free to mix and match materials and go outside the boundaries of the crafts in this book. After all, it's your big day—or your chance to give something straight from the heart.

Tools and Materials: Sewing

To facilitate the craft-making process, make sure you have the following tools and materials so that you are always prepared for various projects that involve sewing.

Fabric Shears

Make sure you have a good, sharp pair for cutting ribbon, fabric, and lace. Never use fabric shears on wired ribbon or paper because these materials will dull the blade. Use a pair of craft scissors for nonfabric materials.

Embroidery Scissors

These are small scissors used for intricate projects that require delicate cutting in small spaces.

Ruler and Tape Measure

Make sure your measuring tools show both inches as well as centimeters.

Needles

The best hand-sewing needles for projects in this book are 9 or 10 millimeters. For beading projects, use an extra-fine needle.

Thread

Most of the projects in this book call for 40 wt. thread. This thread is strong enough for hand sewing, and it won't break easily like some light-weight threads.

Quick Sewing Stitches

Here's a handy reference for when you need to know how to make the most simple stitches.

Backstitch

1 Make a short stitch.

2 Insert the needle at the beginning of the stitch and bring it out a stitch ahead. The result should resemble machine-stitching; it should look neat.

Slip Stitch

1 Pick up a thread or two of fabric.

2 Run the needle inside the folded edge about ¼" and pick up a thread or two.

Running Stitch

This is the simplest of all stitches.

1 First, pull the needle up through the fabric.

2 Push the needle down through the fabric, spacing the entry and departure point to the desired length.

Basting

This means to use a large running stitch, about 1" long.

Bridal Fabric Guide

• • •

BATISTE	Fine, plain-woven fabric made from various fibers
BROCADE	Heavy fabric woven with a rich, raised design
CHARMEUSE	Satin-finished silk fabric
CHIFFON	Sheer silk or rayon fabric, often layered over heavier, stiffer, and shinier fabrics
CREPE	Light, soft, thin fabric of silk, cotton, or wool with a crinkled surface
CREPE DE CHINE	Silk crepe with a soft drape
EYELET	Cotton fabric with small holes edged with embroidered stitches
FAILLE	Slightly ribbed, woven fabric of silk, cotton, or rayon
GEORGETTE	Sheer, strong silk or silky clothing fabric with a dull crepe surface
MOIRÉ	Silk or rayon, finished so as to have a wavy or rippled surface pattern
ORGANZA	Sheer, stiff fabric of silk or synthetic material
SATIN	Smooth fabric made of silk or rayon
SHANTUNG	Heavy fabric with a rough, nubby surface, made of spun wild silk
TAFFETA	Crisp, smooth, plain woven fabric with a slight sheen
TULLE	Fine net of silk, rayon, or nylon
VELVET	Soft fabric made of silk, rayon, or nylon with a smooth dense pile and plain underside

Lace Glossary

• • •

ALENÇON	Net background with a solid design and needlepoint lace
BRUSSELS	Delicate lace with subtle patterns
CHANTILLY	Floral or scroll designs on a mesh-like pattern
CLUNY	An open design made with fine linen thread
FRENCH	Machine-made lace fabrics made to look like handmade French lace
GUIPURE	Heavy needlepoint lace with large patterns
RENAISSANCE	Heavy, flat lace of various stitches joined with tape
SCHIFFLI	Machine-made delicate floral embroidery
SPANISH	Flat design of roses on a mesh background
VENISE	Needlepoint lace of foliage or geometric designs

Decorative Ribbon Guide

• • •

GROSGRAIN	Woven ribbon with a crosswise pattern
JACQUARD	Ribbon with an intricately woven pattern, often with a tapestry look
METALLIC	Ribbon made with shiny or iridescent metal fibers for a sparkled look
ORGANDY	Sheer and often iridescent ribbon made of contrasting colored yarns
SATIN	Available in single or double-faced; sometimes has a feather or picot edge
SHEER	Plain, print, or striped almost transparent ribbon, often with a thick thread woven along the edge
TAFFETA	Crisp, smooth plain-woven ribbon with a slight sheen
TWILL	Ribbon with diagonal parallel lines
WIRE EDGE CRAFT RIBBON	Ribbon with soft wire woven into the edge to help it hold its shape

Choosing Fabrics

Once you have the right sewing tools for crafting projects, you'll need to select the correct fabric for your piece. What's important is that you use your imagination and go with what fits your personal style. Use the chart on page 4 as a directory for which fabrics are most appropriate for your or your loved one's wedding.

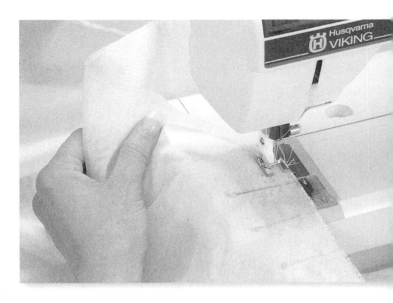

Tools and Materials: Florals

Before you start arranging, get prepared! The tools and materials that are good to have on hand will make the floral projects in this book all the more easy to create. After you find the supplies you need to create projects in this book, investigate the Flower and Foliage Glossary to determine which flowers are right for your arrangement.

Cable Ties

Available at your local hardware store, these are found in many lengths and are ideal for securing hand-tied bouquets.

Chenille Stems

These are similar to pipe cleaners and are used in securing bows and for strengthening stems. They consist of bendable, twistable heavy wire and a material that makes the wire able to allow water to pass through.

Floral Preservatives

Find floral preservatives at your local florist. They contain vital nutrients to help your flowers stay fresher, longer. A type of floral preservative is Chrysal Clear.

Handy Hints

- Allow plenty of time to complete sewing projects.
- Use good tools. They will help you save on time and give you top-notch results.
- Test all fabrics you will be using in a project: Can they withstand moisture? How do they handle when ironed? Should they be pre-washed? Are they dry-clean only?
- Always buy more fabric than you need in case you make a mistake or make more than one of a particular project.

Floral Picks

Wooden floral picks come in several sizes and are useful in securing bows in bouquets and in extending stem lengths.

Floral Wire

This wire comes in different weights, or gauges. Floral wire is used to strengthen stems and bind flowers together.

Floral Tape

Floral tape is used to wrap floral stems and secure flowers together. Available in white and dark and light green, floral tape can be found at your local florist.

Garden Gloves

Great for stripping thorns; wear garden gloves to clean stems of unwanted leaves.

Floral Foam Tape

Available in white or green, floral foam tape comes in various widths. It is used to wrap stems and secure arrangements.

Water Tubes

These are filled with water and used to add fresh flowers to silk or dried bouquets as well as to potted plants. Water tubes are available in various lengths based on the size of your project and where they will be placed in the arrangement.

Wire Cutters

You'll need these to cut thin-stemmed silk flower stems or dried material. For heavier stems, a stronger pair of cutters may be necessary.

See pages 8–9 for the Flower and Foliage Glossary.

How to Preserve Your Wedding Flowers

There are many ways to preserve the flowers from your bouquet, ceremony, or reception arrangements. Flowers can either be air-dried, dried in silica gel, or preserved through an advanced process called freeze-drying. Air-dried and freeze-dried flowers are dried in silica gel without their stems.

Air-Drying

There are several methods of air-drying flowers, including hanging them upside down in a dark, dry, and well-ventilated spot. When dry, the flowers will be smaller than they were originally. Color may be lost and the petals and leaves will appear wrinkled. Most flowers dry between five days and two weeks.

Silica Gel

Silica gel is available in most craft stores. A powder that dries flower heads to look as if new within several days, the gel absorbs moisture from the flowers while supporting their natural shape. Silica gel can be reused several times. The process must be checked daily so the flowers do not overdry and become brittle.

Freeze-Drying

Freeze-drying is a relatively new and advanced drying process that can preserve a flower almost indefinitely. Freeze-dried flowers keep their shape and color, can be used easily in arrangements, and the stem can remain. Simply take the flowers you wish to have freeze-dried to a local florist who specializes in this process. The freeze-drying process can keep your wedding bouquet looking as beautiful as the day you carried it with you down the aisle.

How to Preserve Your Wedding Gown

No other dress will hold as much value as your wedding gown. Whether you choose to keep it for yourself or for your daughter to wear on her wedding day, be sure that it is properly cleaned and stored so that it preserves well.

- Find a dry cleaner that offers wedding gown cleaning services and send your gown to be cleaned one to six months after your wedding day.

- Wedding gowns should be packed with acid-free tissue paper in between the folds of the dress and in the bodice to prevent wrinkles.

- Place the gown in a storage box (preferably a cedar chest, no brown or plastic boxes) to protect from light, dust, and acid. Do not seal the box: The gown needs air circulation, or otherwise the fabric will dry out.

- When handling the gown after a significant amount of time has passed, wear white cotton gloves to keep oils from your hands from affecting the dress.

Flower and Foliage Glossary

Here's your guide to the most popular wedding flowers. Use this glossary to find out when your favorite flowers are in season and the range of available colors.
Note: Please see color insert for a color version of this glossary.

Acacia
Acacia is a soft, yellow flower with wonderful foliage for a distinctive look whether it is fall or springtime. It is best from October through March.

Alstroemeria
Alstroemeria is a trumpet-shaped flower with an array of flower clusters at the top of the stem. It is a favorite and affordable wedding flower available in a variety of colors. This abundant flower stem is available year-round.

Baby's Breath (Gypsophila)
This ball-shaped flower is a wonderful airy accent to all wedding bouquets. It is available year-round in white and shades of pink.

Button Mums
A favorite for fall weddings, this flower is very hardy. Mums can withstand hot temperatures and be without water for hours. They are available year-round.

Carnation
Carnations are round, large headed flowers that can tolerate hot temperatures for summer weddings. With an endless color selection, carnations are popular flowers available year-round at an affordable price.

Caspia (Limonium)
Caspia is a delicate, light accent flower that is available year-round. With a trace of blue, caspia is great for a garden look bouquet. It is easy to arrange and dries well too.

Coffee
This crisp, dark green foliage is becoming a new favorite in wedding arrangements. The waxy leaves are abundant on a soft woody stem.

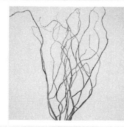

Corkscrew Willow
Corkscrew or curly willow is a favorite for dramatic wedding designs. These branches are available year-round and in various lengths. The tips of the branches are an ideal accent in bouquets.

Daisy Mums
Daisy mums are favorites for fall as well as spring weddings. This crisp looking flower is available year-round and is inexpensive.

Delphinium
Delphinium is a tall and heavy flower-clustered stem that comes in white and shades of lavender, purple, and pink. Available year-round, this elegant flower is popular in hand-tied bouquets.

Eucalyptus
Eucalyptus dries attractively, is easy to arrange and is popular in long trailing bouquets. The leaves have a bluish green to silvery gray cast and are available year-round.

Eucalyptus, Seeded Feather
This type of eucalyptus is lighter and airier than the traditional variety and is becoming increasingly popular among brides. This foliage is also a favorite for drying.

Freesia
Freesia is among the most fragrant of flowers. This beautiful, elegant, bell-shaped flower is available year-round and is a delicate addition to bridal bouquets.

Gardenia
This abundantly fragrant flower is a classic wedding flower. Off-white in appearance, it can be used during any season. Gardenias have a large open blossom and are an elegant choice for any bouquet.

Gerbera Daisy
Gerbera daisies are bright, colorful flowers available in a rainbow of colors. This round, vibrant daisy is available year-round in both large and miniature varieties.

Heather
This long-stemmed flowering branch is a dramatic addition to long, trailing bouquets. Heather is available from November to April in white, lavender, and pink.

Hydrangea
The full and abundant hydrangea is available from March through September. This elegant flower is bright, delicate, and can be easily dried. It is available in lavender, white, and green.

Ivy
Ivy is available with medium to dark green leaves and also with variegated leaves for unique designs. This foliage is a favorite in wedding design and is suited equally for elegant ceremonies and garden weddings.

Leatherleaf Fern
Leatherleaf is the most common and affordable foliage. It is dark green in color and can be found year-round.

Lemonleaf (Salal)
A popular foliage option, lemonleaf has broad, dark green leaves. It is available year-round.

Lily, Asiatic
This star-shaped lily is a favorite in wedding design and enhances any bouquet with color and style. Asiatic lilies come in a wide array of colors and can be found year-round. They do not have a fragrance.

Lily, Casa Blanca
Casa Blanca lilies are elegant, classic, white blooms perfectly suited for weddings. Casa Blancas are fragrant flowers and are available year-round.

Lily, Stargazer
This regal and extremely fragrant flower is a favorite for its large bloom and brilliant colors of white and pink with red accents. It is available year-round.

Orchid, Dendrobium
Dendrobium orchids are butterfly-shaped orchids on a long, flowing stem. This flower is wonderful for cascading bouquets and can be found year-round.

Plumosa
This dark green foliage adds a delicate, lacy look to any arrangement. It is very affordable and available year-round.

Queen Anne's Lace
This round white flower is available year-round. It is a romantic filler flower for wedding bouquets, adding a Victorian touch to any design.

Rose
The rose is a classic choice among brides. Its soft and fragrant bloom makes it an elegant choice for any bridal bouquet. Color selection is almost endless. While roses are available year-round, they are most affordable during the summer months.

Rose, Sweetheart
The sweetheart rose is a petite version of the classic rose and a very popular choice among brides for corsages and accents in bridal bouquets. Sweetheart roses are available year-round but are most affordable during the summer months.

Ruscus, Italian
Italian ruscus has small, green, waxy leaves on multibranching stems. Available year-round, it is an elegant accent foliage in any arrangement.

Sprengeri (Asparagus Fern)
Sprengeri is an elegant, lacy accent foliage for all wedding designs. It is dark green and available year-round. Sprengeri can be used as filler foliage and is also great in long trailing bouquets.

Statice
This very vivid flower is popular as filler. Statice can be used in fresh or dried bouquets and is available in purple and white. It is grown year-round.

Stephanotis
This traditional wedding flower is a favorite in bridal bouquets. Stephanotis blossoms are white, fragrant, and star-shaped. It is available year-round.

Strawberry Bush (Leptospermum)
The dramatic, heavy, woodsy look of this flower makes it a favorite addition to winter bridal bouquets. Strawberry bush is a durable flower that appears in white and shades of pink and red. It is available from September through June.

Tulips
The tulip gives a bright, fresh, springtime feeling to any wedding. It is not recommended during the summer months or for hot days because it will wilt. Color selection is endless and it is available October through May.

Waxflower
Waxflower clusters are a popular alternative to baby's breath for creating a fresh new look in bridal bouquets. Their delicate and vivid waxy petals are shaped like small daisies in true white, pink, or lavender. January through May are the best months for availability.

Yarrow
This striking, dried-looking flower is available fresh and can be dried easily. It is generally available in shades of yellow and is a great choice for fall weddings.

Bowmaking Basics

*B*ows are everywhere! Often a part of wedding bouquets, accessories, corsages, and decorations, here's a foolproof course on how to create beautiful bows.

Get Started:
Ribbon on the bolt • Scissors • Floral wire

1 Begin by pinching the ribbon (still on the bolt) between your fingers approximately 12" (or more than 12" if desired) from the end of the ribbon. This end piece of ribbon will become the first streamer of the bow.

2 To make the center loop of the bow, twist the ribbon with your fingers and form a small hoop.

3 Pinch the ribbon together in the center with your beginning streamer.

4 Continue to hold the bow in the center and twist the leading part of your ribbon.

5 Make a larger loop that will become the start of your actual bow. The size of the loop will determine the width of your bow. As you complete the loop, bring the ribbon back to the center of the bow.

6 Twist the ribbon in the center before beginning each new loop. Keep making loops from side to side until your bow is as full as desired. Four to five loops on a side are a common size.

7 Keep holding the bow in the center with pinched fingers. Cut your ribbon from the bolt to approximately the same length as your starting streamer.

8 Secure your bow by threading a floral wire through it. Pull the wire evenly through the bow, bring the wire ends to the back of the bow, and twist tightly around the center of the bow.

9 You have finished your bow! If you want to add more streamers, cut a piece of ribbon about twice the length (but not exactly) of the existing streamers. Streamers usually look better when they are of varying lengths.

10 Pinch the center of the additional ribbon streamer and secure it with the wire holding the bow together. Adjust the loops attractively on both sides and trim the ends of the streamers with a diagonal or V-cut.

∽ This technique is used in the Wedding Wishes Card Cage, Bride and Groom Thrones, and Bow Bouquet projects.

Ribbon Rules

$\mathcal{F}$eel like creating a homemade bouquet? Try one of these ribbon techniques for creatively wrapping the stems of your bouquet for an extra hint of sophistication and romance.

Get Started:
12" of ribbon or wired ribbon • 3 2" corsage pins (or more if your ribbon is wider than 2")

Fancy Wrap

1 Place your ribbon under the stems at the bottom of the bouquet.

2 Wrap the ribbon around the stems to the front of the bouquet and twist.

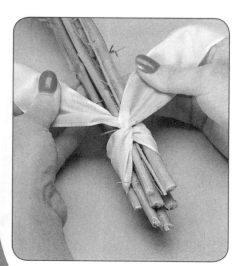

3 Continue to wrap underneath the stems, bringing the ribbon forward and twisting it all the way up the stems of the bouquet until you reach the base of the flowers.

4 Tie off the ribbon at the top with a knot.

5 Finish off the ends of the streamers with an angled cut.

NOTE: If you are using a wired ribbon as shown, you can arrange the streamers as desired.

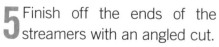

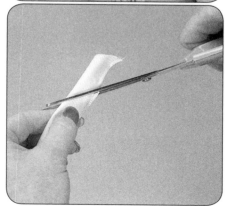

Tailored Wrap

1 Trim the sharp ends off three 2" pearled corsage pins.

2 Cut 12" of ribbon or a length of ribbon that will allow you to wrap the bouquet stems completely, about four to five times. Begin by holding one end of the ribbon securely against the stems, then start wrapping the ribbon around the stems tightly.

3 Continue wrapping the ribbon until the remaining end is ready to be anchored.

4 Fold the end of the ribbon under for a finished look and secure with the first corsage pin. Insert the corsage pin securely at a downward slant.

5 Add the remaining corsage pins along the width of the ribbon until it is totally secure. More corsage pins may be needed if your ribbon is wider than 2".

Wiring Flowers

$\mathcal{T}$his easy technique is found in several projects in this book. A fundamental skill for any florist to know, you can learn how simple it is from the instructions below.

Get Started:
6" floral wire • Flower of your choice • Floral tape

1 Insert a 6" floral wire into the base of any flower head and pull it through.

2 Leave equal lengths of wire on both sides of the flower's base.

3 Pull the ends of the wire down and in line with the stem to begin the wrapping process.

4 Begin the wrapping process using floral tape. (Floral tape becomes tacky and adheres to itself as it is stretched so it does not have a wrong side.) Hold the flower with one hand and tape in the other. Stretch and pull the tape downward.

5 Twist the stem with the thumb and forefinger of one hand. As you twist, the tape should cover the stem snugly, overlapping on its way down the stem.

6 Wrap the ends of the wire and press tape snugly up and around to cover any exposed wire.

∞ This technique is used in the Ivy Pew Décor and Wedding Wishes Card Cage projects.

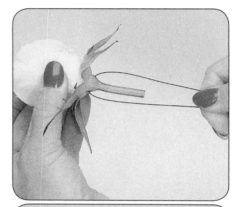
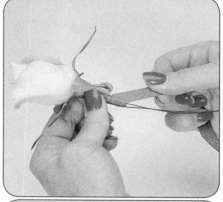

Part Two

Wedding Décor

MATERIALS

Origami paper
in assorted colors

Origami Place Settings

Cranes mate for life and serve as an important symbol in the Japanese wedding tradition. When you fold 1,001 origami cranes, you'll enjoy a long married life together with much good fortune. Use these classy, elegant cranes to dress up reception tables. Use as place settings, position them randomly throughout the reception hall, or hang them from a wedding arch.

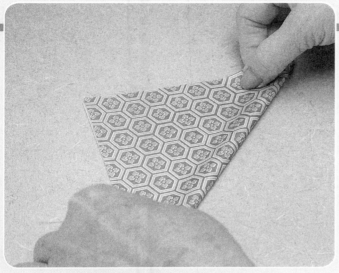

Fold Paper into a Triangle

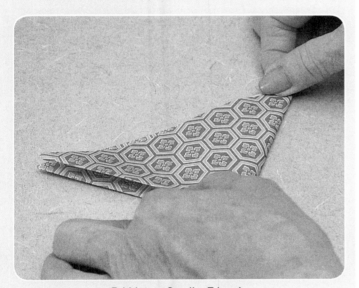

Fold into a Smaller Triangle

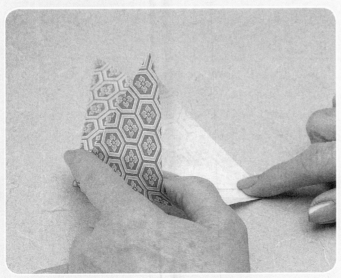

Open Flap

1 Fold a square sheet of origami paper diagonally in half, lining it up corner to corner to form a triangle.

2 Fold the paper again into a smaller triangle.

3 Lay the paper open to the first triangle and open the flap.

4 Flatten the flap to a square and turn the paper over.

Continues

17

5 Open up the other flap and flatten to a square. You should now have a perfect square.

Open Second Flap

6 Fold one corner of the square so that the edge is lined up with the center line. See the figure below for guidance.

Fold First Corner

7 Repeat Step 6 with the other flap to form a triangle in the center.

Fold Second Corner

Complete Four Corners

8 Flip the paper over and repeat Steps 6 and 7 for the other two flaps.

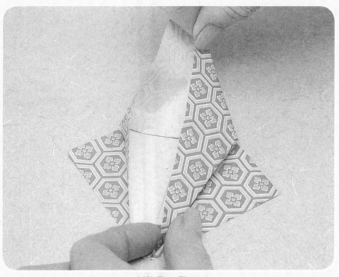

Lift Top Flap

9 Lift the top flap on the open end and fold it upward.

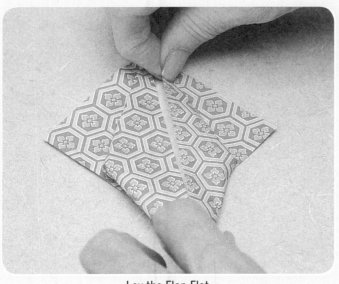

Lay the Flap Flat

10 Lay the flap flat, creating a diamond shape.

Continues

11 Flip the paper over and repeat Steps 9 and 10 on the other side.

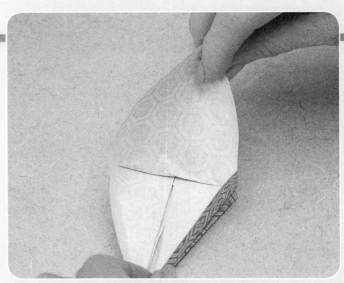

Create Diamond Shape

12 With the open end pointing toward you, fold in one flap so that the edge lines up with the center line.

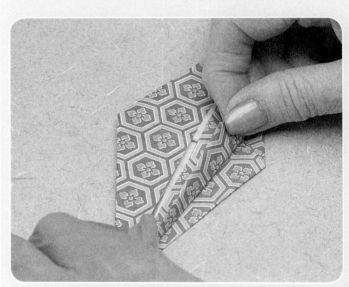

Fold in One Flap

13 Repeat Step 12 for the other flap so both flaps are lined up along the center.

14 Flip the paper over and repeat Step 12 for both flaps on the other side.

Complete All Center Flaps

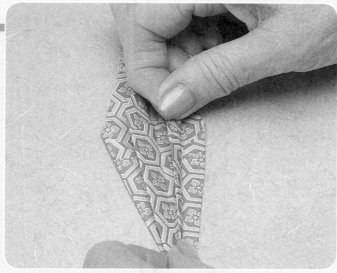

Turn Right Flap

15 Turn the right flap to the left and lay it flat.

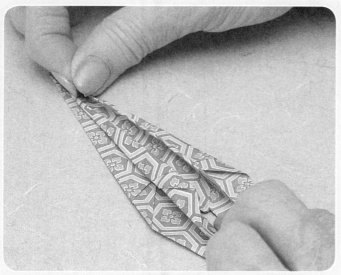

Turn Left Flap

16 Repeat Step 14 on the other side and lay it flat.

Make Wings

17 Pull the bottom flat flap all the way up to form the first wing. Repeat on the other side.

18 Invert one of the upper tips to form the head.

19 Pull back the opposite tip to form the tail.

20 Gently pull the wings apart to form the body, finishing the piece.

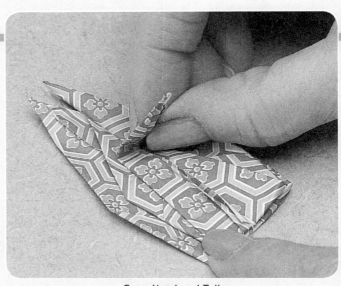

Form Head and Tail

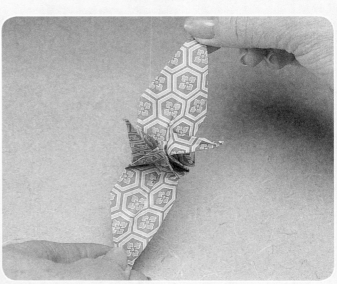

Form the Body

Completed Origami Place Settings

3 roses

1 stem waxflower

1 stem acacia

1 stem strawberry bush

1 stem baby's breath

1–2 stems plumosa

1–2 stems coffee foliage

Large floral foam igloo

Floral Frosting

Dress up your cake—not with frosting—but with flowers! For a stunning presentation, match flowers you choose for the ceremony and reception to those that will sit on your cake!

1 Soak the floral foam igloo in water for approximately fifteen minutes or until saturated.

2 Cut short sprigs of coffee foliage and insert to cover the base of the cage. The diameter of the cage with greenery should be slightly larger than the diameter of the cake top.

3 Continue to insert coffee sprigs, layering up toward the center. Insert sprigs in the top and add more sprigs if necessary to create an even dome shape.

4 Cut sprigs of plumosa and insert them randomly throughout the floral cage.

Add Greenery

Layer Coffee Foliage

Add Plumosa

Add Roses

5 Cut three roses leaving 3" stems and insert around base.

6 Cut various lengths of strawberry bush and insert into the floral foam, placing the tallest one on top.

7 Cut various lengths of baby's breath and insert the pieces randomly throughout the arrangement.

Add Strawberry Bush

Add Baby's Breath

8 Cut various lengths of waxflower and fill pieces in randomly as desired.

9 Cut various lengths of acacia and add as desired.

NOTE: The cake top can be made up to forty-eight hours in advance of the wedding. Put arrangement in a low pan with 1" of water to keep it hydrated. Store it in the refrigerator or in a cool, dark place. If you want to embellish the cake flower arrangement further, cut small clusters of waxflower, acacia, or baby's breath and place them around each cake tier. Be careful not to dig into the icing. You can also ask the bakery that makes your cake to place the flowers on the cake for you.

Add Waxflower

Add Acacia

Completed Floral Frosting

MATERIALS

Foam topiary form

Green spray paint

Clay pot or other decorative plant container

Floral adhesive

1 small silk ivy bush

Sphagnum moss
(and water to soak the moss)

Floral picks

8–10 branches seeded eucalyptus

Greening pins

5–8 stems privet berry

5–8 stems pepper berry

6 stems heather

3 stems caspia

Leaf shine spray

18 roses

3 stems baby's breath

3 branches curly willow

Decorative ribbon

Statuesque Centerpiece

Create this stunning topiary with fresh flowers that will later dry naturally, making a quaint keepsake for this joyous occasion. Create this one special centerpiece for the bride and groom's reception table only and create similar ones for the guest tables using different flower selections.

Continues

Paint Topiary Form

1 Using green spray paint, paint the stem of the foam topiary form. (This will make it so the stem blends into the arrangement.)

Glue Topiary Form to Pot

2 Apply floral adhesive to the base of the foam topiary form where it comes into contact with the clay pot.

3 Press the topiary into the clay pot firmly and hold it until the glue seems secure.

Prepare the Base

4 Soak the sphagnum moss in water until it is thoroughly wet.

5 Gently wring out pieces of moss and place them on top of the base of the topiary to cover the foam form. If necessary, floral adhesive can be used to attach the moss securely.

Drape Ivy Around Topiary

6 Wind a stem of silk ivy around topiary, working from the bottom.

NOTE: If the stem will not go into the foam form, poke a hole in the foam with a floral pick.

7 Secure the stem in the hole with floral adhesive. Press the other end of the stem into the foam base through the moss. Use a floral pick to create a hole and floral adhesive if needed to secure the stem.

Cover Topiary Ball with Ivy

8 Add a second stem of ivy, securing one end at the top of the topiary ball and the other end at the bottom of the topiary ball. Continue adding ivy stems until the ball is covered.

Add Ivy to Topiary Base

9 Insert additional stems of ivy into the topiary base. Drape them over the sides of the pot.

Continues ➤

10 Cut sprigs of seeded eucalyptus and insert them into the topiary ball until it is completely covered.

11 Use the floral pick to create holes for inserting stems and add floral adhesive to hold the stems securely.

Add Eucalyptus

12 Add sprigs of seeded eucalyptus to the topiary base and secure them with greening pins.

Insert Eucalyptus in Topiary Base

13 Cut sprigs of privet berries. Insert them into the topiary as desired.

Add Privet Berries

Add Pepper Berries

14 Cut sprigs of pepper berries. Insert them into the topiary form as desired.

15 Cut sprigs of heather. Insert them randomly throughout the topiary. If necessary, use a floral pick to create a hole and apply floral adhesive to secure the stems.

16 Cut sprigs of caspia. Use floral adhesive to insert them randomly in the topiary.

Add Heather

Add Caspia

Continues

17 Spray the entire topiary with leaf shine.

NOTE: Spraying with leaf shine will help preserve the filler materials, keeping them from drying out and preserving the colors.

Spray Leaf Shine

18 Cut stems of roses, leaving 4" and remove the thorns.

19 Use a floral pick to make a hole and insert the roses randomly around the topiary ball.

20 Use floral adhesive to secure the roses, especially those angled down. Also add a rose or two to the base.

Add Roses

21 Cut stems of baby's breath and insert them randomly throughout the topiary ball and base. Use the floral pick and floral adhesive if necessary.

Add Baby's Breath

Add Curly Willow

Attach Ribbon

22 Cut stems of curly willow long enough to easily wrap around the topiary ball and insert as desired.

NOTE: Stems from the curly willow may be cut short to stick out or cut longer to be wrapped around and inserted into the foam at both ends.

23 Cut lengths of ribbon and fold one end over to form a loop.

24 Use a greening pin to attach the loop to the base of the topiary ball. Arrange the streamers as desired.

25 Feel free to add extra streamers as shown in the figure below.

NOTE: Most of the topiary can be made a week before the wedding, with the roses and baby's breath added 24 hours in advance of the reception. Store the centerpiece in a cool place and avoid direct sunlight.

*Completed
Statuesque Centerpiece*

MATERIALS

Dry sahara foam
(one brick)

Open floral cage

¼"-wide floral foam tape

Silk ivy bushes
(one large bush with long
trailers and one small bush)

Green chenille stems

4–6 stems silk baby's breath

Floral wire

Floral pick

Green floral tape

2½"-wide sheer ribbon

3–7 stemmed silk lilies

3–9 silk roses, open

Corkscrew willow branches

Ivy Pew Décor

Bring a splash of color to the pews with this ivy arrangement. Brilliant with red roses and lovely lilies, add to the ivy a sheer ribbon bow for a special finish. Contact the ceremony site for placement and attachment requirements for this quaint decoration.

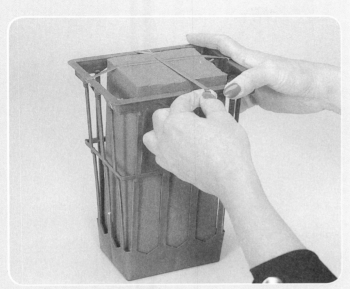

Prepare Floral Cage

Insert Ivy

Arrange Ivy

1 Insert the dry foam brick into the cage and tape it into place with floral foam tape.

2 Insert the large ivy bush into the side of the cage approximately two-thirds of the way up. Make sure the stem is pushed in firmly at an angle.

3 Open the bush with your hands and unfold the individual stems in an attractive manner around the cage, making sure the longest trails of ivy are at the bottom.

Continues ➜

4 Cut sprigs of ivy from the second ivy bush and insert them into the sides of the cage to completely hide the cage.

5 Add more sprigs as needed to cover the entire cage. Both the sides and front of the cage should be entirely covered with ivy, leaving the back uncovered so it can rest flat against the pew.

Cover the Cage

6 Loop a chenille stem through the center bars of the back of the cage just below the top and twist them together.

NOTE: Although this hanger may not be necessary during the ceremony (depending upon various facility accommodations), the hanger will allow the arrangement to also be displayed on a wall, stairway, or candelabra.

Attach Hanger

7 Cut sprigs of baby's breath and place them randomly throughout the ivy.

Add Baby's Breath

Add Bow

8 Make a standard bow with extra streamers. Wire the center with floral wire, and attach to a floral pick by wrapping with floral tape.

9 Insert the completed bow by pushing the floral pick into the dry foam slightly above the center of the cage in the front.

10 Fluff and arrange the loops of the bow. Allow the ivy to intertwine with the loops.

Add Lilies

11 Cut individual lily blossoms from the stems with varying lengths of stem remaining.

12 Arrange the lilies randomly in the bouquet using shorter flowers in the middle and longer stems at the top, on the bottom, and sides.

Add Roses

13 Cut rose stems to varying lengths of 6" to 10" and place as desired.

NOTE: The color of the roses should be the accent color used throughout the wedding and/or coordinate with the bridesmaids' dresses.

Continues

14 Cut willow branches as desired and add randomly to the arrangement.

Add Willow Branches

Completed Ivy Pew Décor

Candelabra Variation »

Use the same pew decoration to adorn a candelabra. Candelabras may be rented or may be available at a church. Simply hang the pew decoration on the candelabra with chenille stems for a striking display.

MATERIALS

Birdcage
(wires should be spaced so
as to allow large cards enough
room to pass through)

Wire cutters

1 silk baby tears bush

Green chenille stems

1 silk rose bush
with open roses
(2 or more roses per stem)

Foam floral cage

Floral adhesive

Butterfly decorations
(optional)

Double-sided woven ribbon

Wedding Wishes Card Cage

Take an ordinary birdcage and add to it velvety roses, colorful butterfly décor, and elaborate woven ribbon to create a card holder inspired by a lush garden. Use the striking cage as a centerpiece for your gift table.

Continues

1 Determine how the swing is attached and remove it. If necessary, use wire cutters to snip the attachment.

2 Cut three stems of various lengths from the baby tears bush.

3 Wrap the stem ends around the top of the birdcage and twist them securely around the top finial.

NOTE: Stems must be long enough to drape over the top half of the birdcage.

4 Intertwine the stems around the wires of the birdcage, draping them around the top half of the cage.

NOTE: Avoid twining stems over the door, since the door will need to be opened to remove envelopes after the reception.

5 Bring the ends of the baby tear stems down around the sides of the birdcage and continue winding the stems around. If necessary, use green chenille stems to secure the stems to the birdcage, trimming or tucking the ends out of sight.

Remove Swing

Add Baby Tears

Intertwine Stems

Secure Stems

Add Baby Tears to Birdcage Base

Complete Greenery

Insert Large Rose

Note: Make sure there are enough spaces in the cage for people to pass standard-size envelopes through to the inside.

6 Placing baby tear stems around the base of the birdcage is up to you. If desired, wrap the stems around the base of the birdcage and intertwine the stems up the sides.

7 Continue adding baby tear stems until the desired effect is reached. To fill holes, trim small stems and add them by intertwining them with the longer stems or wrapping them into place with a chenille stem. Remember to leave the door and surrounding area free and clear of greenery.

8 Cut one large open rose from the bush, leaving approximately 2½" of stem.

9 Insert the rose into the front side of the floral foam cage.

10 Cut two smaller roses from the bush and leave approximately 1" of stem.

11 Insert one rose on each side of the larger rose, placing one higher than the other.

NOTE: Remember to keep the floral foam arrangement compact so it can fit through the birdcage door.

Add Smaller Roses

12 Cut a small rosebud from the bush, leaving approximately 3" of stem. Insert the rosebud in the center of the other three roses, keeping it straight.

Insert Center Rosebud

13 Cut sprigs of rose leaves and insert them into the floral foam cage as greenery. Fill in with the leaves until the cage is covered.

Add Leaves

Add Adhesive to Floral Cage

14 Squeeze a generous amount of floral adhesive onto the bottom of the floral cage arrangement. Let the glue set for a few minutes so that it can become tacky.

Add Adhesive to Birdcage

15 Squeeze a medium amount of floral adhesive onto the center of the floor of the birdcage. Allow the glue to set for a few minutes so that it can become tacky.

Place Arrangement in Birdcage

16 Gently push the arrangement through the birdcage door, center it in the middle of the birdcage, and glue it securely into place.

17 Carefully cut the wire from the butterfly and glue it to one of the rose petals.

NOTE: The birdcage door may be closed at this time. Wrap a branch of garland around the closure to secure the door until after the wedding.

Continues

18 Place a double stem of open roses through the hanger and around the top of the birdcage so the stems hang down on either side.

19 Twist the stems to arrange the flowers as desired. Do not wire or glue them in place at this time.

20 Insert a second double stem of roses through the opposite side of the birdcage hanger.

21 Drape the stems over the top of the birdcage perpendicular to the first stem. Press down on all the rose stems and mold them to the shape of the birdcage.

NOTE: If you want to use other flowers besides roses, any multibranch flower will do. Or, wire single flower stems to the birdcage with chenille stems.

22 Wrap a single stem rose securely around the top of the birdcage on top of the other stems and arrange as desired.

23 When the flowers are arranged as desired, cut small lengths of chenille stem and twist them around the flower stems where they touch the birdcage.

Add Rose Stem to Birdcage Top

Add Second Rose Stem

Add Single Rose

Secure Flowers

Add Bow

24 Trim any excess wire. Bend the wires back under the foliage to hide the ends. Glue a butterfly to one of the roses.

25 Use 4 yards of ribbon to make a bow (see the Bowmaking Basics technique on page 10). Make the bow loops in varying sizes to drape over the top of the birdcage.

26 Cut an additional 36" of ribbon and make two extra streamers. Wire the streamers into the bow with a green chenille stem.

27 Anchor the bow to the birdcage by wrapping chenille stems securely around the top of the cage. Bend the ends into the foliage to conceal them.

28 Pull half of the bow loops through the birdcage hanger. Arrange the loops and streamers as desired. Trim the ends of the streamers.

Completed
Wedding Wishes Card Cage

MATERIALS

Plumosa

Hand towel

Paddle wire

Baby's breath

Coffee foliage

Caspia

Strawberry bush

Waxflower

Alstroemeria

Petite water tubes

Floral Garland

Create this dazzling garland for the doorway of your ceremony or reception venue—or use it to liven up doors, archways, windows, or tables. Vivid greenery is used in combination with alstroemeria, waxflower, strawberry bush, baby's breath, and caspia for a decoration so perfect for draping anywhere!

Strip Thorns

Begin Garland

Add Stems

1 If the stems of plumosa are thorny, use a hand towel to safely strip the thorns off.

2 Crisscross two stems of plumosa and wrap paddle wire around the center to secure the stems together. This will create one end of the garland.

3 Add more stems of plumosa.

Continues

4 Layer each stem or stems (depending on desired fullness) one on top of the other.

Layer Stems

5 Secure the stems of plumosa by holding the garland with one hand and wrapping the paddle wire around it with the other.

NOTE: The paddle wire should be wrapped over some branches, but others can be loose and free.

Wrap Stems with Wire

6 Cut any excess stem with clippers as you form the garland.

Cut Stems

Finish End of Garland

7 Continue adding plumosa until a desired length is reached.

8 Finish the end of the garland by adding the last plumosa stem in a crisscross manner.

9 Make a knot with the paddle wire to secure it at the end of the garland.

Add Baby's Breath

10 Cut branches of baby's breath and space them along the garland.

11 Wrap the stems into the garland with paddle wire.

Add Coffee Foliage

12 Cut stems of coffee foliage and lay them underneath the entire length of the garland.

13 Wrap paddle wire from one end to the other to secure the stems to the garland.

NOTE: Longer stems are easier to wrap into the garland and add volume.

NOTE: Wrap the paddle wire continually from one end of the garland to the other as more materials are added. You will not cut the wire until the very end.

Continues ➤

14 Cut pieces of caspia and randomly place them along the garland. Secure them by wrapping with paddle wire from one end to the other.

Add Caspia

15 Cut branches of strawberry bush and place along the garland. Wrap with paddle wire to secure.

Add Strawberry Bush

16 Add stems of waxflower to the garland and wrap with paddle wire.

Add Waxflower

Add Alstroemeria

Secure Flowers

17 Cut alstroemeria leaving approximately 8" long stems and insert pieces into water-filled tubes.

18 Place the flowers in various directions along the garland. Wrap paddle wire around the water tubes to secure them in the garland.

19 Wrap the paddle wire once more around the completed garland to secure everything.

20 Wrap wire under individual flowers and foliage as needed. Cut the wire and bend the ends into the center of the garland.

NOTE: The garland can be made up to forty-eight hours in advance of the wedding. To prevent wilting, lightly mist the garland. Coil it inside a dark plastic bag with a few air holes. Store it in a cool, dark place.

Completed
Floral
Garland

MATERIALS

1"- to 1$^{1}/_{2}$"-wide plastic or wooden ring

White floral tape

1 yard of $^{5}/_{8}$"-wide white satin ribbon

1 silk mini carnation for each napkin ring

Floral adhesive

3 silk ranunculus blossoms for each napkin ring

2 silk yarrow clusters for each napkin ring

1 silk statice stem for each napkin ring

1 silk baby's breath stem for each napkin ring

Mini Bouquet Napkin Ring

Coordinate your flower selections with those that you use for these simple napkin rings. Inexpensive and easy to create, you'll brighten up every place setting with these small bursts of color.

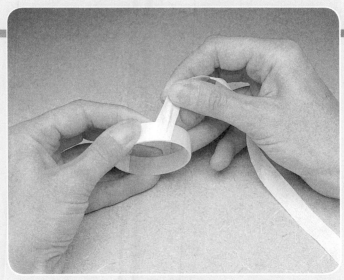

Wrap Ring

1 Wrap the entire ring with white floral tape, overlapping the tape slightly so it covers the whole surface.

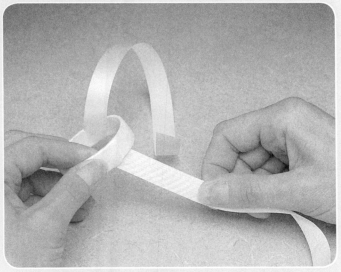

Add Ribbon

2 Wrap the entire ring with satin ribbon, leaving approximately 9" worth of ribbon streamers at the beginning and end.

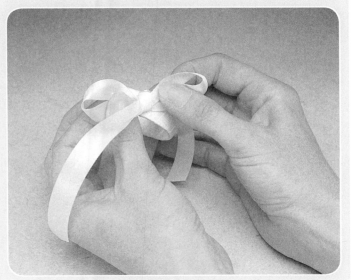

Tie Ribbon Ends

3 After wrapping, tie the ribbon streamers snugly and make a shoestring bow. Trim the ribbon ends diagonally.

Continues

4 Cut stems of miniature carnations and separate the individual blossoms from the stem base to make the flowers less bulky for gluing. Save the leaf stems for later.

Cut Carnation Blossoms

5 Place a small amount of floral adhesive on the back of the carnation and wait a few moments until the glue gets tacky. Attach the carnation to the center of the napkin ring bow.

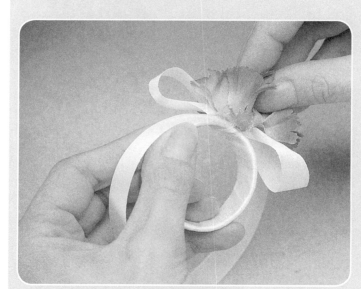

Attach Carnation

6 Glue three ranunculus blossoms around the carnation.

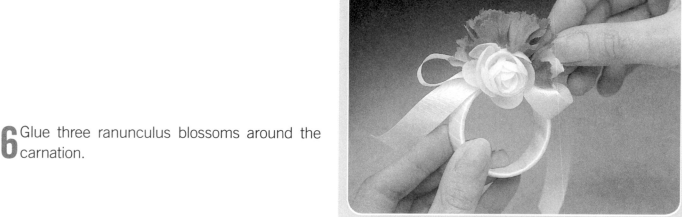

Add Ranunculus

Add Yarrow

Add Statice

Add Baby's Breath

7 Glue two clusters of yarrow on either side of the flower cluster.

8 Glue individual buds of statice to fill in open spaces.

9 Fill in remaining open spaces with baby's breath.

10 Embellish the floral cluster by adding leaves from the carnation stems.

Add Greenery

Completed Mini Bouquet Napkin Ring

MATERIALS

48" × 60" of fabric per chair
(heavy, nonwrinkle upholstery-
grade brocade, cotton chintz or
moiré; no sheer or satin)

Common pins

Iron

1"-wide fusible seam tape

Safety pins

No. 40 ivory satin ribbon
(2 yards for each chair)

Coordinating wide, fancy
satin ribbon for bow
(5–6 yards for each chair)

1 small silk ivy bush

4–6 silk rose sprays
(2 or more flowers per stem)

Cable ties

Wire cutters

2" and 1½" corsage pins

Chenille stems

Bride and Groom Thrones

Dress up the newlyweds' chairs! Use elegant fabric to create a dramatic look for the honored couple. Decorate with fancy satin ribbons
and lush silk roses for a hint of romance.

1 To make sure the fabric is the proper size for the chair being covered, drape the fabric evenly over the chair. Make sure the raw edges of the fabric touch the floor all the way around the chair and there is at least 6" of excess fabric on all sides.

2 Trim the fabric if necessary. Pin up a 1" hem on all sides of the fabric and iron flat.

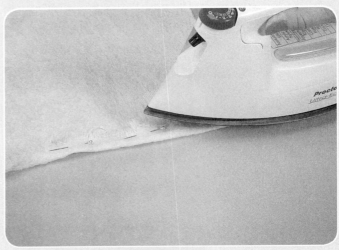

Measure Fabric

3 Remove the pins and fold the fabric edge again to form a 1" seam with a finished edge. Pin and iron flat.

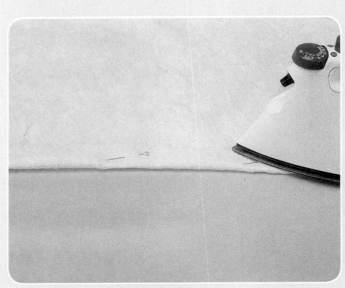

Create Seam

4 Remove the pins and cut lengths of fusible seam tape to lie along the edges of the fabric seam.

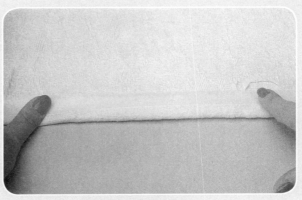

Place Seam Tape

Page
16

Page
23

Page 27

Page 34

Page
57

Page
78

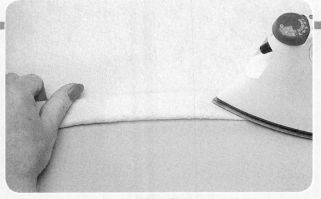

Fuse Seam

5 Fold the fabric once more so that the fusible seam tape is underneath the folded edge.

6 Pin the seam if necessary and iron it until the fusible seam tape is activated and secures the finished fabric edge.

Drape Chair with Fabric

7 Drape the hemmed fabric over the chair and arrange so that all of the edges are touching the floor.

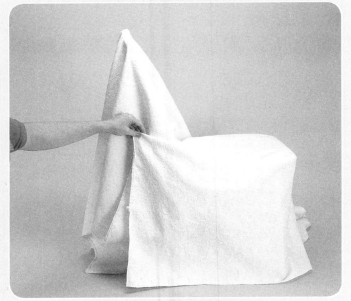

Create Side Panels

8 Pull the fabric from one front chair leg flush with the chair back so that the fabric hangs evenly across the front and side of the chair. Pin the fabric to hold it in place. Repeat this for the opposite side.

Continues

9 Pull any excess fabric that is draped over the back of the chair forward to cover the side seam. Pin in place. Repeat this for the opposite side.

Cover Side Seam

10 Pull the two center back folds together and overlap them. Secure underneath with safety pins.

Overlap Back Folds

11 Wrap the no. 40 satin ribbon around the chair back and tie it with a knot. Leave enough ribbon to form streamers and allow them to graze the floor.

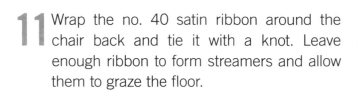

Wrap Ribbon Around Chair

Add Bow

12 Using the Bowmaking Basics technique on page 10, make a large bow out of the satin ribbon. For the groom's chair, pin the bow to the back of the chair over the knot. The groom's chair is finished! Do not secure a bow to the bride's chair yet. Proceed to the next step.

Begin Bouquet

13 To make the floral bouquet, start with the small ivy bush and add three stems of roses.

14 Arrange the roses in a triangle pattern and weave the ivy stems between the flowers.

Gather Flowers

15 Add three shorter stemmed roses and wrap all the stems securely with a cable tie.

16 Cut off the excess tie end. Trim the stems to approximately 8" to 10" if necessary.

Wrap Stems

17 Starting at the base of the bouquet, wrap the stems tightly with no. 40 satin ribbon.

Secure Ribbon

18 At the top of the stems, trim the ribbon, fold over the end, and pin ribbon securely with two or three corsage pins.

19 Attach the bow from Step 12 to the front of the bouquet with a chenille stem.

Attach Bow to Bouquet

Attach Bouquet to Chair

20 Slide the bouquet stems inside the chair ribbon.

21 Pin individual flowers and ivy stems to the chair fabric where necessary to secure the bouquet in place.

Completed
Bride Throne

Part Three

Accessorize!

MATERIALS

3 yard x 19 ½" tulle

Hand-sewing needle

White 40 wt. thread

¾"-wide headband
(without teeth)

¼ yard satin fabric

¼"-wide double-sided tape

Glue gun

Common pins

Fifty pearl stems

Fabric glue

10 yard satin cording

⅝"-wide grosgrain ribbon

Velcro

7" of ⅜"-wide elastic

The Bride's Veil

What's more exquisite than a veil you wear for the wedding, which transforms into a headpiece for the reception? A stunning accessory that will flatter your face, complement your dress, and match your personality will surely make you feel more beautiful on your special day.

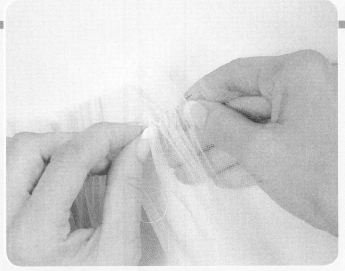

Baste Tulle

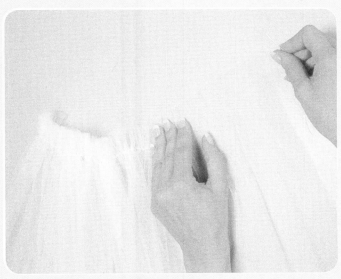

Gather Tulle

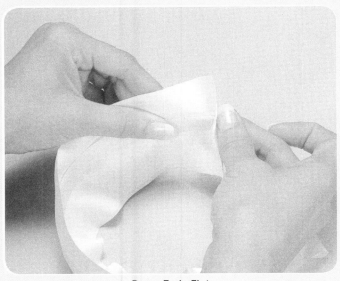

Press Ends Flat

1 Hand baste a running seam along the entire length of the tulle 1" from the top. Do not cut the thread. See page 3 for Quick Sewing Stitches.

2 To form the veil, tie a knot at one end of the basting thread and pull the thread at the other end of the tulle to gather it until it is only 7" wide.

3 Tie the thread and cut off any excess. Set the veil aside.

4 Measure the length of the headband and add approximately 1", then measure the width of the headband and add approximately 2".

5 Cut the satin fabric to match these measurements.

6 Place a small piece of double-sided tape on the inside of the headband at each end at the bottom.

7 Center the fabric on the headband and fold the ends of the fabric over onto the tape. Press the ends flat.

Continues

8 Place double-sided tape along the center of the inside of the headband from one end to the other.

9 Fold one side of the fabric onto the tape and press until smooth.

10 Trim any excess fabric and then hot glue the ends.

11 Fold the fabric on the other side. Adjust and pin in place. Trim any excess fabric along the edge of the headband.

12 Use a small amount of hot glue to attach the ends of the satin to the headband.

13 Begin to hot glue the satin into place along the inside length of the headband, removing the pins as you glue. Adjust and trim any excess fabric.

14 Cut the satin into thirty 2" × 4" strips.

15 Fold the wrong sides together lengthwise and pin together.

Place Double-Sided Tape

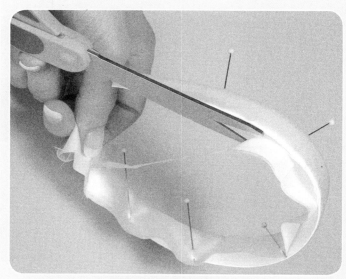

Adjust and Pin in Place

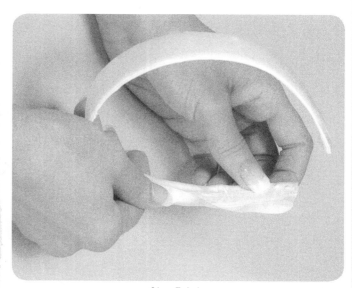

Glue Fabric

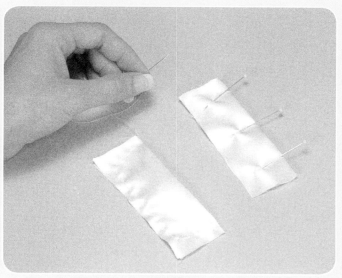

Pin Together

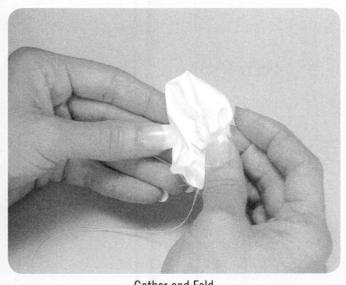

Gather and Fold

16 Hand baste the fabric in a long U-shape pattern, rounding off the corners as you stitch. Allow a ¼" seam allowance. Do not cut the thread until the rosebud is complete. See page 3 for Quick Sewing Stitches.

17 Pull the thread to gather the fabric together. Overlap the gathers one on top of the other to form a small rosebud.

Choose the Right Veil for You

Veils come in all lengths and styles. Some edges are unfinished or trimmed with ribbon or satin cording. The entire veil can be embellished with sew-on pearls, crystals, sequins, beads, silk flowers, or embroidery. Customize your veil to match the style of your wedding dress by adding decorative details or simply by changing the length. Here is a guide to a few of the different lengths you can select for your veil:

Ballet or **Waltz** veils fall somewhere between the knees and the ankles.

Cathedral veils are quite long, falling 3½ yards from your headpiece, trailing several feet behind you.

Chapel veils extend to the floor 2½ yards from your headpiece. There is just enough fabric to gently gather around your feet.

Elbow veils fall 25" to your elbows.

Fingertip veils extend to the end of your fingers. This popular length is particularly beautiful with gown style dresses.

Flyaway or **Madonna** veils are multilayered and barely brush the shoulders. Made with stiffened fabric, they slightly lift away from the body.

Blusher veils are short and made only of one layer. They are worn over the face to add mystery. They can be worn with any style or length of veil described above.

18 Secure the rosebud by stitching the base, tightly wrapping the thread around the rosebud and tying it off.

19 Cut approximately forty-five pearl stems in half.

20 Use fabric glue to secure three pearl stems in the center of each rosebud. Repeat Steps 14–19 to create thirty rosebuds.

21 Begin hot gluing the rosebuds onto each side of the headband until they meet in the middle. Overlap each rosebud slightly.

22 Cut forty 3" lengths of cording. Make a loop then hot glue the ends together.

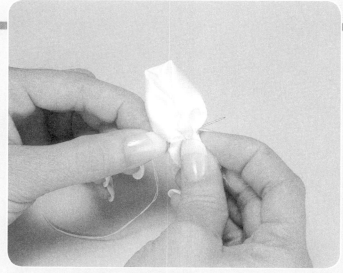

Secure Rosebud

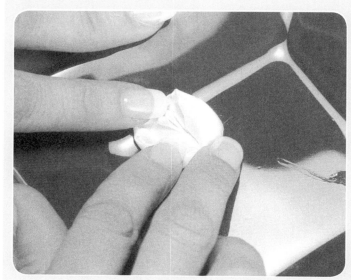

Cut Pearl Stems

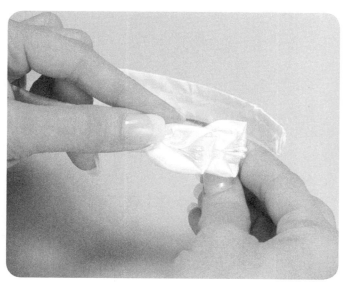

Attach Rosebuds

Create Cording Loops

Attach Cording Loops

Attach Loops to Center of Headband

Create Rosebud Center

23 Hot glue a cording loop on each side of every other rosebud, working from the ends of the headband up to the middle.

24 At the center of the headband, hot glue five cording loops on each side so that there are ten loops forming a bow.

25 Cut five pearl stems in half and hot glue one pearl stem to the center of each loop.

26 Hot glue two rosebuds together, end to end.

27 Cut a 3" length of cording. Hot glue one end to the back of the two rosebuds where their ends intersect.

28 Wrap the cording tightly around the intersection three times.

Continues

. . . The Bride's Veil

29 Cut any excess cording. Secure the end with hot glue on the back of the rosebuds.

30 Place the two rosebuds in the center of the headband and hot glue them into the intersection of the ten loops of cording. Hold the rosebuds in place until the glue has bonded.

REMEMBER: If you wish, you can hot glue loops of cording next to every rosebud.

31 Cut two 1" pieces of satin cording. On each side of the headband, 2½" from each end, make a small loop for hairpins. Secure with hot glue.

32 Place double-sided tape along the inside of the headband from end to end.

33 Cut 15" grosgrain ribbon.

34 Fold the end of the ribbon ½" and glue in place.

35 Press the ribbon onto the inside of the end of the headband. Cut any excess ribbon. Make sure to keep the hairpin loops free.

Attach Rosebuds

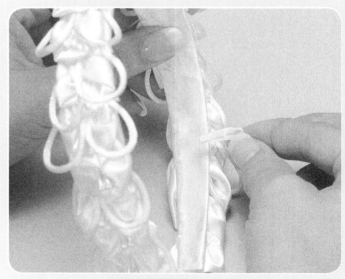

Create Hairpin Loops

Add Grosgrain Ribbon

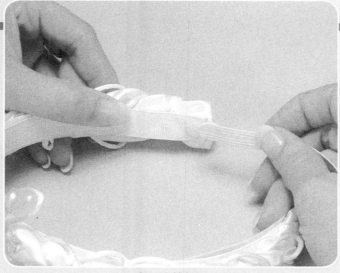

Attach Velcro

Attach Veil

36 Cut two small Velcro circles and hot glue them onto the inside of the headband at each end. Do not take the Velcro apart.

37 Hot glue each end of the 6½"-piece of elastic to the Velcro circles to create a detachable veil band. When you have glued the elastic to the Velcro, then you can pull it apart.

38 Run a line of hot glue down the middle of the elastic and attach it to the veil. The veil should now easily detach with the Velcro circles.

DON'T FORGET: Take your headpiece and/or veil to your hairstylist to make sure it fits comfortably on your head and complements your hairstyle. Secure the headband to your head by sliding hairpins through the cording loops on each side.

Completed Bride's Veil

MATERIALS

Two floral igloo cages

Floral adhesive

Floral wire

Wire cutters

Silk cord

30–48 roses

Flora Lock

Waxflower

The Flower Girl's Pomander

This flower arrangement is an enchanting alternative bouquet for the flower girl. The pomander hangs on a braided silk cord perfect for a pair of small hands. After the wedding, allow the flowers to dry and send off the pomander with your flower girl as a reminder of your love for her having been a part of your wedding.

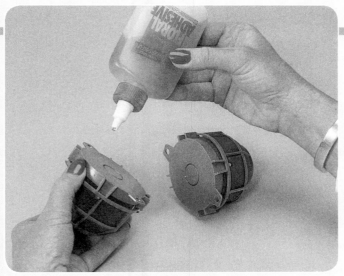

Prepare Igloo Cages

1 Soak the igloos in water for approximately fifteen minutes.

2 Completely cover the bottom of both igloos with adhesive. Let them sit for one to two minutes until adhesive gets tacky.

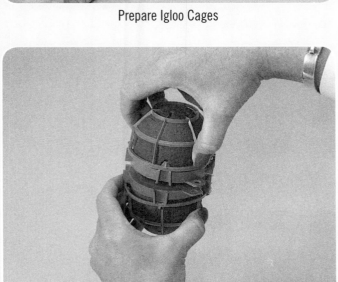

Join Igloo Cages

3 Press both igloos together to form a sphere, making sure the eyelets are lined up to match. Wipe off any excess glue with a damp towel.

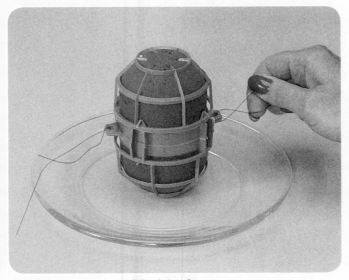

Wire Igloo Cages

4 To secure the igloo cages together, put floral wire through the eyelets on both sides, pull tight and twist.

5 Trim the ends of the wire with wire cutters and bend the twisted ends into the cage to hide them.

6 Lay the igloo on its side and pass the cording through the frame of the igloo just beside the eyelet. Tie it off with a knot.

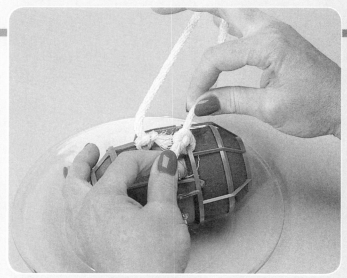

Add Handle

7 Cut the stems of eight roses leaving approximately 2" of stem and remove the thorns.

Insert Base Roses

8 Place a rose in each end of the pomander. Next, place roses in a circular formation around the ball. Spray Flora Lock on all the rose stems to hold them securely in the floral foam.

NOTE: In order to cover the entire center frame of the pomander, some roses should be inserted at an angle.

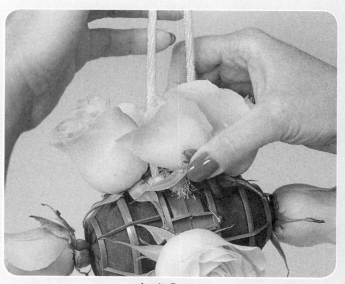

Angle Roses

Fill in with Roses

Add Waxflower

9 Continue to insert roses around the pomander until it is completely covered. Use Flora Lock to secure the stems.

NOTE: An alternate method of giving your pomander a nice dense look while saving money on the number of roses needed is to make good use of greenery. The number of roses needed may also depend upon how open the blossoms are.

10 Cut small sprigs of waxflower approximately 3" long, stripping the foliage from the last inch of the stem.

11 Insert waxflower randomly around the roses. Outer stems of waxflower may be trimmed with scissors if a more compact look is desired.

NOTE: The rose pomander can be made three days in advance and hung in the refrigerator until four hours in advance of the wedding. Hang the pomander in a cool, dry place out of the sunlight for those few hours to allow the roses to open to full bloom. After the wedding, the pomander can be dried naturally.

*Completed
Flower Girl's Pomander*

MATERIALS

½ yard satin fabric

Quilt batting

16-gauge clear vinyl plastic or lightweight clear plastic vinyl

Tape

White 40 wt. thread

Common pins

Bridal pearl trim

Glue gun

⅛"-wide satin ribbon

¼"-wide sheer satin ribbon

Bridal rose appliqué

Poly fiber-fill

Wedding invitation

Ring Cushion

Easy and fun to create, you'll want to keep this ring bearer's pillow to cherish for years to come. Featuring your wedding invitation, you can relax knowing that the wedding bands are in a safe place!

Sew Plastic to Satin Fabric

Pin Quilt Batting

Sew Pillow

1 Cut two 11" × 11" squares of satin fabric and one 11" × 11" square of quilt batting.

2 Cut the clear plastic 1" larger than your invitation on all sides.

3 Center the plastic on the right side of the satin fabric and tape it down.

4 Sew the plastic to the fabric on three sides leaving the top side open so the invitation can be inserted later. Do not sew over the tape. Remove each piece of tape as you sew. See page 3 for Quick Sewing Stitches.

5 Pin the square of quilt batting to the wrong side of the satin fabric with the plastic sewn to it.

6 With the right sides of the satin fabric facing each other, pin the squares together.

7 Stitch around the pillow using a ¼" seam allowance. Leave a 6" opening on one side for turning inside out and stuffing the pillow.

8 Cut all the corners diagonally. Trim the seam allowance and turn the pillow right side out. Press the pillow with a cool iron if necessary.

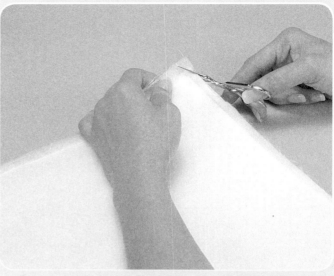

Cut Corners

9 Hot glue the pearl trim around the edges of the plastic to cover up the stitching lines.

10 Put the hot glue on the back of the trim to avoid melting the plastic.

NOTE: To prevent the hot glue from getting on the fabric at the top edge of the plastic, insert a small piece of paper into the pillow pocket.

Glue Pearl Trim

11 Cut a 22" piece of sheer satin ribbon. Cut a 22¼" and a 14" piece of satin ribbon.

12 Fold all three ribbons in the center, and glue them to the top left corner of the plastic on the edge of the pearl trim.

13 Randomly tie knots along the streamers and tie on the wedding rings.

Attach Streamers

Tie Shoestring Bow

14 Cut two 14" lengths of sheer satin ribbon, and tie a shoestring bow. Repeat with the ⅛"-wide satin ribbon.

15 Glue pieces to the top left corners of the pillow over the streamers. Trim the ribbon ends diagonally.

Add Ribbon Loops

16 Cut two 4" pieces of sheer satin and satin ribbons.

17 Make ribbon loops and glue the ends together with a small amount of hot glue.

18 Attach the loops placing one on top of the other at the center of the bow using a small amount of hot glue.

Attach Rose

19 Cut one small rose from the pearl trim and hot glue it to the center of the bow.

20 At the center of the top of the pillow just above the plastic, glue the bridal appliqué onto the fabric.

Add Bridal Appliqué

21 Use small amounts of poly fiber-fill to stuff the pillow. Stuff the corners of the pillow first. Fill the pillow gradually; this will keep the pillow from looking lumpy.

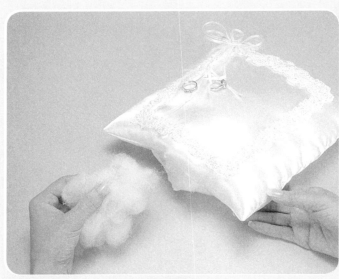

Stuff Pillow

22 Slip stitch the opening in the pillow closed. Tie the ends of the thread together and cut excess thread. See page 3 for Quick Sewing Stitches.

NOTE: Give your ring bearer a set of symbolic rings for his trip down the aisle and the real rings to your maid or matron of honor and the best man.

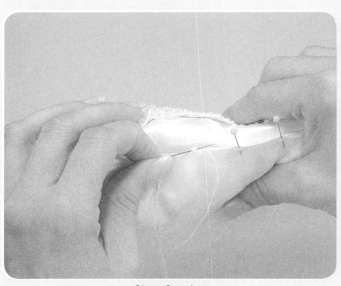

Close Opening

This day I will marry my best friend,
Lisa G. Brewer
daughter of
Mr. & Mrs. Edwin Brewer
and
Christopher C. Carson
son of
Mr. & Mrs. Homer L. Carson
on Saturday, the ninth of December
two thousand and one
at three o'clock in the afternoon
Mt. Moriah Church
129 Crestview Ave.
Florence, Ky. 45776

Completed Ring Cushion

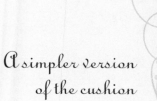

*A simpler version
of the cushion*

MATERIALS

Hair comb

Floral adhesive

1 stem baby's breath

3 sweetheart roses

Sweetheart Hair Comb

There's no need for complicated hairstyles when there are sweetheart roses nestled in your hair. Even on hair that has been pulled up, this sweetheart rose hair accessory adds just the right amount of color.

Add Glue to Comb

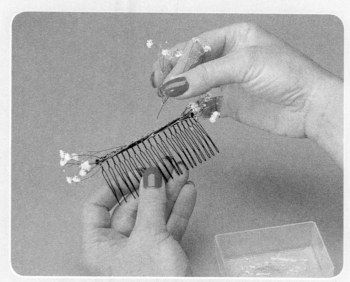

Add Baby's Breath

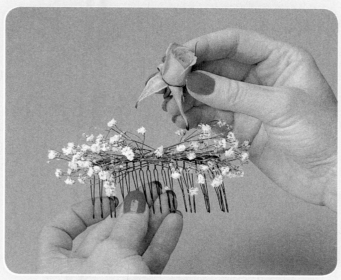

Add Sweetheart Roses

1 Apply a line of floral adhesive to the entire length of the hair comb. Let the adhesive set for approximately one to two minutes (until it gets tacky) before adding the flowers.

2 Put a small amount of floral adhesive in a small dish so it can start to get tacky.

3 Cut small pieces of baby's breath and dip the stems in the adhesive.

4 Layer the stems of baby's breath until the comb is covered.

5 Cut individual sweetheart rosebuds off at the base of the flower.

NOTE: Be sure to keep the outer green leaves around the buds.

6 Dip three buds in the adhesive and attach them to the center of the hair comb in a triangle.

NOTE: The comb can be made up to three days in advance of the wedding. Store it in the refrigerator in a plastic bag with a few holes for ventilation to keep it from mildewing. After the wedding, just allow the flowers to dry naturally and save the comb as a keepsake of this special day.

MATERIALS

33" × 72" organza

White 40 wt. thread

Iron

1 yard guipure lace

Flat-back rhinestones

Fabric glue

Hand-sewing needle

Elegant Bridal Wrap

Wrap elegance around you with delicate lace and frothy organza.
To be your most beautiful, drape the wrap at your shoulders or gather
it gracefully with a dainty brooch. Whether you leave the material
simple or trim with lace, beads, or pearl embellishments, you'll know
what accents your dress best.

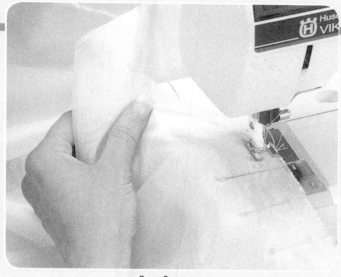

Sew Organza

1 With the right sides of the organza together, fold it in half lengthwise and pin. Stitch a ¼" seam allowance, leaving a 6" opening on the long side for turning it inside out, as shown below.

Trim Seam

2 Using scissors, trim any excess organza close to the seam allowance along the three completely stitched sides of the wrap.

3 Turn the organza right side out and press it with a warm iron. Stitch the 6" opening closed. See page 3 for Quick Sewing Stitches.

Pin Guipure Lace

4 Pin the guipure lace to each end of the sheer wrap.

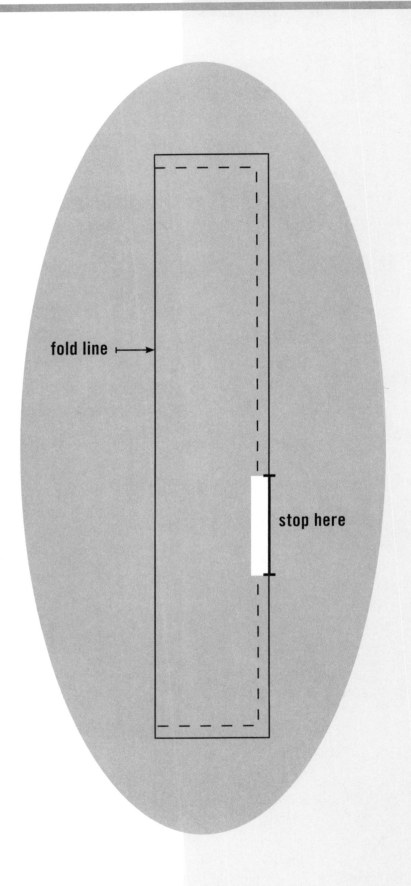

fold line

stop here

Glue Rhinestones

5 Cut away any excess lace. Following the shape of the motifs, hand-stitch the lace in place.

6 Place a rhinestone on your index finger with the flat side facing upward.

7 Place a dab of fabric glue on the flat side.

8 Decorate the motif with rhinestones according to your taste.

Completed Variation of Elegant Bridal Wrap

Flower and Foliage Glossary

Here's your guide to the most popular wedding flowers. Use this glossary to find out when your favorite flowers are in season and the range of available colors.

Acacia
Acacia is a soft, yellow flower with wonderful foliage for a distinctive look whether it is fall or springtime. It is best from October through March.

Alstroemeria
Alstroemeria is a trumpet-shaped flower with an array of flower clusters at the top of the stem. It is a favorite and affordable wedding flower available in a variety of colors. This abundant flower stem is available year-round.

Baby's Breath (Gypsophila)
This ball-shaped flower is a wonderful airy accent to all wedding bouquets. It is available year-round in white and shades of pink.

Button Mums
A favorite for fall weddings, this flower is very hardy. Mums can withstand hot temperatures and be without water for hours. They are available year-round.

Carnation
Carnations are round, large headed flowers that can tolerate hot temperatures for summer weddings. With an endless color selection, carnations are popular flowers available year-round at an affordable price.

Caspia (Limonium)
Caspia is a delicate, light accent flower that is available year-round. With a trace of blue, caspia is great for a garden look bouquet. It is easy to arrange and dries well too.

Coffee
This crisp, dark green foliage is becoming a new favorite in wedding arrangements. The waxy leaves are abundant on a soft woody stem.

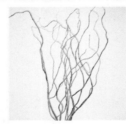

Corkscrew Willow
Corkscrew or curly willow is a favorite for dramatic wedding designs. These branches are available year-round and in various lengths. The tips of the branches are an ideal accent in bouquets.

Daisy Mums
Daisy mums are favorites for fall as well as spring weddings. This crisp looking flower is available year-round and is inexpensive.

Delphinium
Delphinium is a tall and heavy flower-clustered stem that comes in white and shades of lavender, purple, and pink. Available year-round, this elegant flower is popular in hand-tied bouquets.

Eucalyptus
Eucalyptus dries attractively, is easy to arrange and is popular in long trailing bouquets. The leaves have a bluish green to silvery gray cast and are available year-round.

Eucalyptus, Seeded Feather
This type of eucalyptus is lighter and airier than the traditional variety and is becoming increasingly popular among brides. This foliage is also a favorite for drying.

Freesia
Freesia is among the most fragrant of flowers. This beautiful, elegant, bell-shaped flower is available year-round and is a delicate addition to bridal bouquets.

Gardenia
This abundantly fragrant flower is a classic wedding flower. Off-white in appearance, it can be used during any season. Gardenias have a large open blossom and are an elegant choice for any bouquet.

Gerbera Daisy
Gerbera daisies are bright, colorful flowers available in a rainbow of colors. This round, vibrant daisy is available year-round in both large and miniature varieties.

Heather
This long-stemmed flowering branch is a dramatic addition to long, trailing bouquets. Heather is available from November to April in white, lavender, and pink.

Hydrangea
The full and abundant hydrangea is available from March through September. This elegant flower is bright, delicate, and can be easily dried. It is available in lavender, white, and green.

Ivy
Ivy is available with medium to dark green leaves and also with variegated leaves for unique designs. This foliage is a favorite in wedding design and is suited equally for elegant ceremonies and garden weddings.

Leatherleaf Fern
Leatherleaf is the most common and affordable foliage. It is dark green in color and can be found year-round.

Lemonleaf (Salal)
A popular foliage option, lemonleaf has broad, dark green leaves. It is available year-round.

Lily, Asiatic
This star-shaped lily is a favorite in wedding design and enhances any bouquet with color and style. Asiatic lilies come in a wide array of colors and can be found year-round. They do not have a fragrance.

Lily, Casa Blanca
Casa Blanca lilies are elegant, classic, white blooms perfectly suited for weddings. Casa Blancas are fragrant flowers and are available year-round.

Lily, Stargazer
This regal and extremely fragrant flower is a favorite for its large bloom and brilliant colors of white and pink with red accents. It is available year-round.

Orchid, Dendrobium
Dendrobium orchids are butterfly-shaped orchids on a long, flowing stem. This flower is wonderful for cascading bouquets and can be found year-round.

Plumosa
This dark green foliage adds a delicate, lacy look to any arrangement. It is very affordable and available year-round.

Queen Anne's Lace
This round white flower is available year-round. It is a romantic filler flower for wedding bouquets, adding a Victorian touch to any design.

Rose
The rose is a classic choice among brides. Its soft and fragrant bloom makes it an elegant choice for any bridal bouquet. Color selection is almost endless. While roses are available year-round, they are most affordable during the summer months.

Rose, Sweetheart
The sweetheart rose is a petite version of the classic rose and a very popular choice among brides for corsages and accents in bridal bouquets. Sweetheart roses are available year-round but are most affordable during the summer months.

Ruscus, Italian
Italian ruscus has small, green, waxy leaves on multibranching stems. Available year-round, it is an elegant accent foliage in any arrangement.

Sprengeri (Asparagus Fern)
Sprengeri is an elegant, lacy accent foliage for all wedding designs. It is dark green and available year-round. Sprengeri can be used as filler foliage and is also great in long trailing bouquets.

Statice
This very vivid flower is popular as filler. Statice can be used in fresh or dried bouquets and is available in purple and white. It is grown year-round.

Stephanotis
This traditional wedding flower is a favorite in bridal bouquets. Stephanotis blossoms are white, fragrant, and star-shaped. It is available year-round.

Strawberry Bush (Leptospermum)
The dramatic, heavy, woodsy look of this flower makes it a favorite addition to winter bridal bouquets. Strawberry bush is a durable flower that appears in white and shades of pink and red. It is available from September through June.

Tulips
The tulip gives a bright, fresh, springtime feeling to any wedding. It is not recommended during the summer months or for hot days because it will wilt. Color selection is endless and it is available October through May.

Waxflower
Waxflower clusters are a popular alternative to baby's breath for creating a fresh new look in bridal bouquets. Their delicate and vivid waxy petals are shaped like small daisies in true white, pink, or lavender. January through May are the best months for availability.

Yarrow
This striking, dried-looking flower is available fresh and can be dried easily. It is generally available in shades of yellow and is a great choice for fall weddings.

Page
92

Page
111

Page
118

Page
132

Page
136

Part Four

Safe Keeping

MATERIALS

1¼"-wide satin wired ribbon

Fusible web or 1"-wide fusible web seam tape

Iron

24" cording with tassel tie

Satin Tote

Use this elegant tote to dress up a bottle of champagne for the bride and groom's table at the reception. Why not use the tote as an envelope holder or favor holder? No matter how it's used, this stylish accessory will add class to the big day.

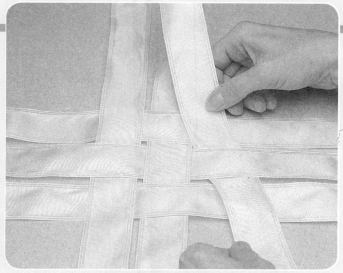

Form the Base of the Pouch

1 Cut six strips of ribbon to the length equaling double the height of the bottle plus 12".

2 Interweave the ribbon by using a simple over-and-under technique with three strips of ribbon vertical and three strips ribbon horizontal.

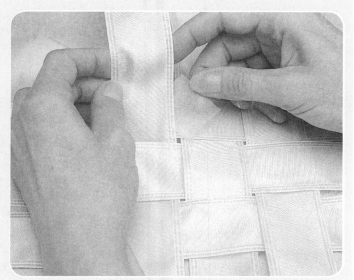

Insert Fusible Web

3 Cut 1" squares of fusible web and insert where the ribbons overlap. To insert a square of fusible web, position it under vertical ribbons where they overlap horizontal ribbons. It is not mandatory to place a piece of fusible web under every overlapping piece. By placing the fusible web under every other square of ribbon, the tote will have a fluffier appearance than if the web is placed underneath every square.

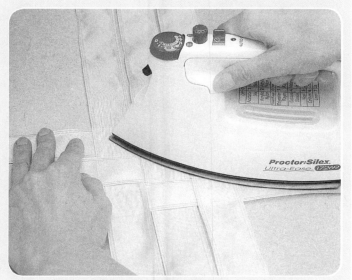

Iron Fusible Web

4 When each fusible web square has been positioned evenly under the overlapping sections of ribbon, press the ribbon with a warm iron to activate the fusible web and adhere the ribbon strips together. The fusible web is placed in a checkerboard manner underneath the overlapping sections of the vertical strips.

Continues

5 Cut eight strips of ribbon 24" long. These pieces will be used to weave the body of the tote.

6 Start the first row by weaving one end of the ribbon through one side of the three vertical strips as shown. Place a square of fusible web under each of the two end squares of the vertical ribbon.

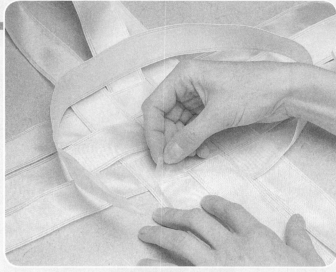

Begin First Row of Tote

7 Iron both squares of fusible web to secure the first row of ribbon.

8 Continue to weave the ribbon around the base on the next side, placing a square of fusible web underneath the center strip of ribbon. As you continue weaving the body of the tote, you will be placing the fusible web underneath every other square of the ribbons creating the rows. One side will be fused under the two outside squares, the second side will be fused under the center square, the third side will be fused under the two outside squares, and the fourth side will be fused underneath the center square.

NOTE: Starting with the second side, you will need to shape the ribbons into a tote.

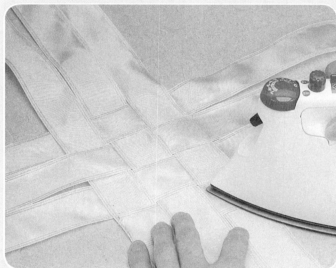

Secure Ribbon

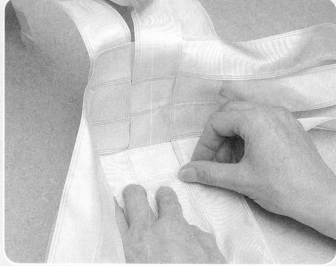

Continue Weaving

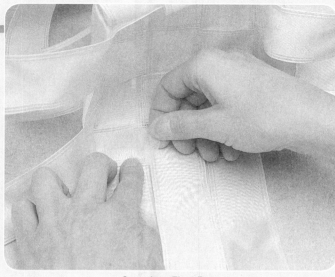

Complete First Row

Begin Second Row

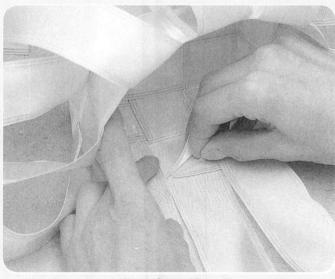

Weave Second Row

9 When you have finished the fourth side of the first row, overlap the end of the ribbon onto the beginning square. Place a square of fusible web underneath it and iron in place.

10 Trim the end of the ribbon if needed.

NOTE: When weaving the ribbon around the body of the tote, lay the ribbons on a flat surface and make sure all the pieces are spaced evenly and tightly.

11 Continuing with the same every-other-square technique, begin the second row. Overlap the end of the second row ribbon over the center strip of base ribbon on the first side. Place a square of fusible web underneath it and iron it in place.

12 Continue weaving and fusing the strip of ribbon in the second row. The first side—the same side row one was started on—will be fused under the center square, the second side will be fused underneath the two outer squares, the third side will be fused under the center square, and the fourth side will be fused underneath the two outer squares.

13 To complete the row, bring the ribbon around to the starting side and overlap the center square with the end of the ribbon. Fuse the end in place and trim if necessary.

Complete Second Row

14 The tote begins to take shape after the first two rows are complete.

Continue Weaving Rows

15 Continue weaving the body of the tote. Rows three (shown in figure), five, and seven are woven and fused the same way as with row one. Rows four, six, and eight are woven and fused the same as with row two.

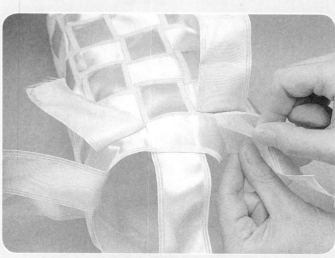

16 Attach the end of the last row of ribbon by overlapping and inserting a square of fusible web. Iron it in place.

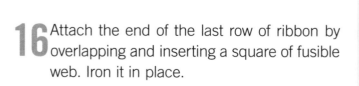

Finish Weaving Top Row

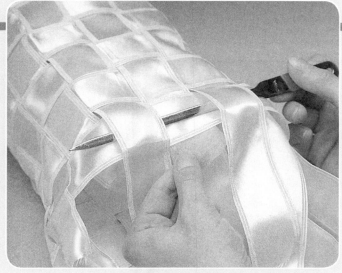

Fuse Top Row of Pouch

17 After the eighth row has been completed, the inner sections of the vertical ribbons need to be fused to the inside of the pouch. Use a letter opener or another tool to simulate the cording passing through the ribbon to avoid fusing a section of ribbon that needs to be left open.

18 Place a square of fusible web between the ribbon sections and iron in place. On the first side, the fusible web will be underneath the center ribbon.

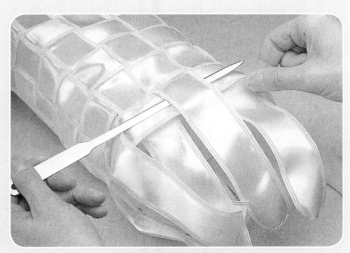

Complete Top Row

19 Continue fusing the inside top of the tote. On the second side, the fusible web squares will be placed underneath the two outer squares as shown in the figure. Continue around to sides three and four, alternating squares.

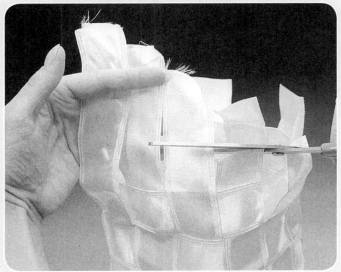

Trim Ribbon Ends

20 Measure and cut the ribbons coming out of the top of the tote to 1". These will be folded over the inside of the tote to form a smooth top edge.

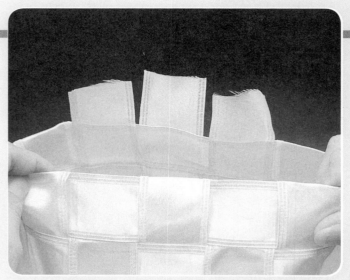

Form Top Edge

21 Bend each ribbon end toward the center of the tote. Alternating squares will either bend over the last row of ribbon or back on themselves.

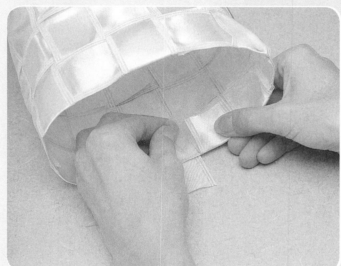

Fuse Ribbons

22 Place a piece of fusible web under each ribbon end and iron in place.

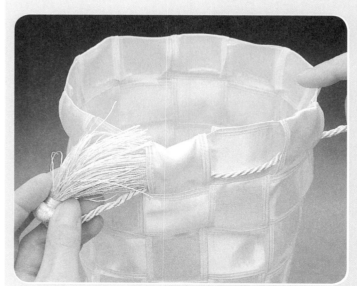

Insert Cording

23 Insert the cording into the top row of the tote by pushing the knot of the tassel through the open sections.

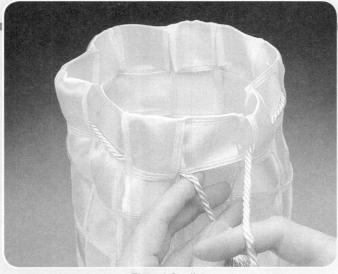

Thread Cording

Complete Pouch Opening

Completed Satin Tote

24 Continue threading cording through the top sections.

25 Continue threading the tassel through the sections until it is wrapped twice around the pouch top.

26 Bring both ends out of the same opening and adjust until the tassels are even.

MATERIALS

Two floral foam bricks

4" × 18" green plastic tray

¼"-wide floral foam tape

Floral adhesive

Unity or pillar candle 10" to 12"

Two 15" taper candles

Lemonleaf (salal)

Leaf shine

Baby's breath

Plumosa

4–5 stems alstroemeria

5–8 stems freesia

Acacia

Unity Candle

Lighting the unity candle during the wedding ceremony is a symbolic and momentous event. Celebrate this union with a gorgeous arrangement of alstroemeria, acacia, freesia, and baby's breath or select your own flowers and greenery for the candle's décor.

Form Base

Tape Floral Foam

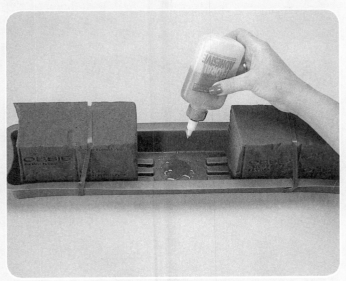

Add Floral Adhesive

1 Soak the floral foam in water until it is completely saturated.

2 Put the floral foam in the tray and cut each brick to fit, leaving an open space in the middle to accommodate the width of the unity candle.

3 Tape the bricks in the tray using floral foam tape.

NOTE: Wrap the tape all the way around the tray and the floral foam. Make sure the tape is slightly off-center to allow room for the taper candles.

4 Place floral adhesive on the bottom of the tray where the unity candle will be placed.

Continues

5 Cover the bottom of the unity candle with adhesive. Wait several minutes so the glue can become tacky and then place the candle firmly down into the tray, making sure it is centered.

Place Unity Candle

6 Push the taper candles into the floral foam firmly, making sure each candle that is inserted is straight.

NOTE: If the candle is not straight or is loose, place floral adhesive on the candle base and inside the hole and reinsert the candle once glue has become tacky.

Place Taper Candles

7 Trim the lemonleaf stems into sprigs and insert them around the lower base of the floral foam. Make sure the leaves cover the tray, all of the floral foam, and the area around the base of the unity candle.

Add Greenery

Add More Greenery

8 Fill in any openings at the base with small pieces of greenery. Spray all the greenery with leaf shine.

Add Baby's Breath

9 Cut small sprigs of baby's breath and insert them randomly between the pieces of lemon-leaf. Feel free to lift leaves to insert the baby's breath stems into the floral foam.

Add Plumosa

10 Cut small sprigs of plumosa and insert them randomly throughout the arrangement.

Continues 103

11 Cut two stems of white alstroemeria, making sure that three or four flowers remain on the stem.

12 Insert one stem at the base of each taper candle.

Surround Candles with Alstroemeria

13 Cut individual blossoms of yellow alstroemeria from the stems and insert as desired across the front of the arrangement.

Add Alstroemeria to Base

14 Cut freesia stems approximately 4" in length and add as desired around the base.

Add Freesia

Add Acacia

15 Cut sprigs of acacia, leaving approximately 4" to 6" of stem, and insert randomly as desired.

NOTE: This arrangement can be made up to two days in advance of the wedding. Store it in a cool, dark place and water regularly. Make sure the candles have good wicks for lighting ease. Loosen the taper candles from the foam before the ceremony to allow them to be picked up easily.

Completed Unity Candle

15" × 15" poster board

String

Pencil

Straight pin

15" × 15" fusible web

1½ yards of 54"-wide
off-white satin

Iron

Wide wired ribbon

Thin accent ribbon

Bow Bouquet

Perfect to carry down the aisle during the wedding rehearsal, this
colorful bow bouquet can be made with satin bows that you collect
at your bridal shower. This will be a special accessory for any bride-
to-be, as this bouquet is easy and fun to make—and beautiful.

Draw Circle

1 Draw a circle 15" in diameter onto the poster board with a pencil. To draw the circle by hand, make a compass by cutting a piece of string approximately 10" long and tying it around a pencil.

2 Measure 7½" along the string and use the remaining end of the string to tie a knot around a straight pin.

3 Insert the pin into the center of the poster board and draw the circle with the pencil, making sure to keep the string taut and the pencil upright as you draw. See figure.

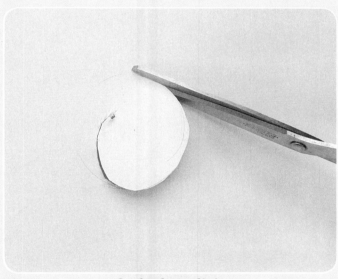

Cut Out Center Circle

4 Using the same technique as in Step 1, draw a circle 2" in diameter in the center of the larger circle.

5 Cut out the center circle.

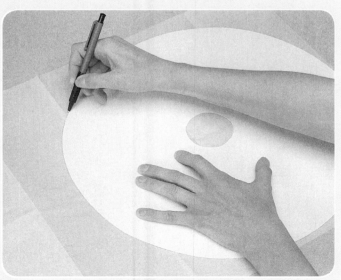

Cut Circle from Fusible Web

6 Place the large poster board circle on top of the fusible web. Trace the outside outline of the circle onto the web.

7 Cut the circle out of the fusible web. Do not cut out the center circle from the fusible web.

8 Cut the satin fabric into a circle. The diameter of the circle should be the same as the width of the fabric (this circle is 54" in diameter). Use the technique from Step 1 to draw the circle.

9 Lay the fabric face down on the ironing board and place the fusible web circle in the center of the fabric circle.

10 Put the poster board circle on top of the fusible web. Make sure the fusible web and poster board circles are lined up before ironing.

11 Using a hot iron on a medium setting, iron the satin until the fusible web attaches the satin and poster board together securely.

12 Using scissors, poke a hole in the center of the fabric covering the 2" hole in the center of the poster board.

13 Cut pie-shaped pieces in the satin within the hole.

14 The pie-shaped pieces already have fusible web on them, so fold them over onto the poster board.

15 Iron the pieces down carefully to form the center hole.

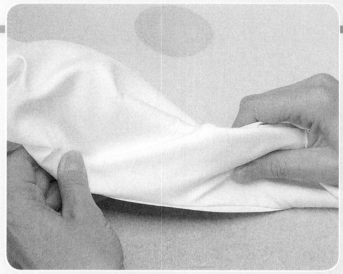

Attach Satin to Poster Board

Cut Out Center Hole

Iron Fabric

Pull Fabric Through Center Hole

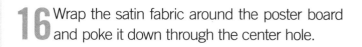Wrap the satin fabric around the poster board and poke it down through the center hole.

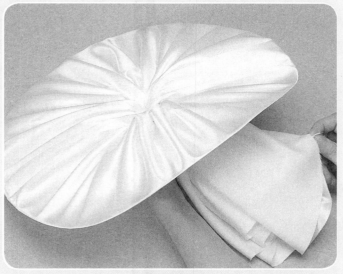

Create Pleats

17 Pull the fabric down through the hole so that pleats form on the top of the bow holder.

Insert Bow

18 To start the bow bouquet, make a large bow out of the wide wired ribbon using the Bow-making Basics technique on page 10.

19 Pull the bow streamers down through the center hole of the holder.

Continues

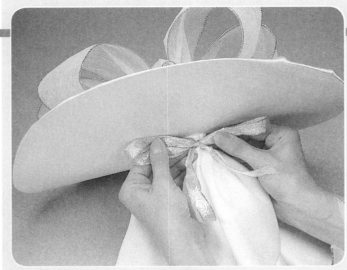

Secure the Bow

20 Underneath the bow bouquet, use the accent ribbon to tie a bow to hold the fabric and large bow in place. See figure.

21 Add the bows one-by-one to the bouquet by pulling the streamers down through the center fabric hole. If a bow does not have any streamers, tie a length of ribbon around it to make a streamer. The accent bow may be untied and re-tied to accommodate additional ribbons as needed. Try taping or pinning bows on the top of the holder, letting the streamers drape off to the sides.

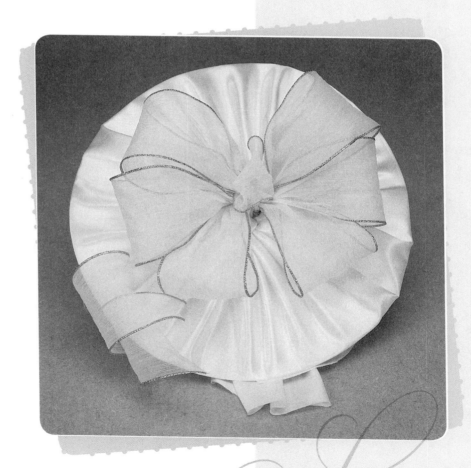

Completed Bow Bouquet

MATERIALS

1½"-wide wired ribbon

Floral foam ring
(9" ring pictured)

Seeded eucalyptus
(dried or fresh)

Clear acrylic gloss spray

Invitation

Pencil

Paper punch

⅝"-wide sheer ribbon

Floral adhesive

Eucalyptus

Dried caspia

Dried baby's breath

Dried statice

Dried German statice

Dried delphinium

Wedding Wreath

Create this keepsake to cherish your wedding day in the years to come. Use an invitation or list your wedding vows as the wreath's center. Substitute dried flowers with preserved ones from your or your bridesmaid's bouquet. This decoration should allow you to look back on your special day with fond memories— so feel free to use anything that will add to the wreath's sentimental value.

Continues

1 Cut a piece of wired ribbon 36" long.

2 Pull the ribbon through the floral foam ring and tie a knot.

3 Trim ends as desired. The size of the floral ring needed for this project will depend upon the size of your wedding invitation.

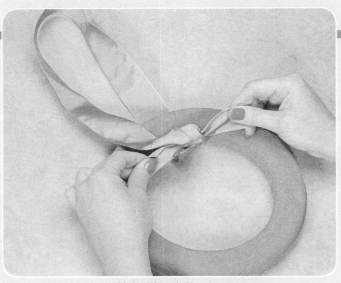

Make Wreath Hanger

4 Cut small pieces (sprigs) of seeded eucalyptus. Use them to start filling in the floral ring.

5 Push the stems into the floral ring at least 1".

NOTE: Push the stems at an angle into the floral foam for added security, so that when the wreath hangs, the stems won't fall out. If any of the stems do not anchor firmly into the floral foam, use a small amount of floral adhesive on the stems before reinserting.

Insert Seeded Eucalyptus

6 When the foam ring has been completely covered with seeded eucalyptus, spray the wreath with clear acrylic gloss.

NOTE: The spraying should be done outside or in a well-ventilated area to avoid inhalation of fumes. Fold the ribbon hanger up behind the wreath when spraying to avoid contact with the ribbon.

Spray Wreath with Clear Gloss

Invitation Placement

7 Place the invitation on top of the wreath, making sure the proportion and shape are desirable.

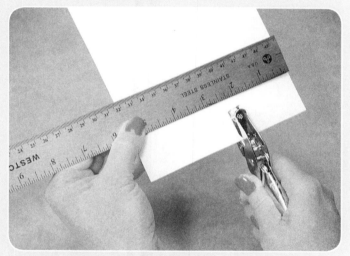

Punch Holes

8 Working from the back of the invitation, measure the card to place two holes each at the top and bottom, 1" apart.

9 Find the center of the invitation and make a small mark ½" on either side of the center-most point. Punch out the holes with a paper punch.

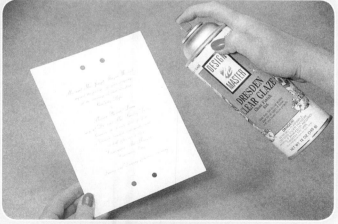

Spray with Clear Acrylic Gloss

10 Spray both sides of the invitation with clear acrylic gloss for preservation.

Continues

11 Cut two 24" lengths of ⅝" sheer ribbon.

12 Thread the ribbon through the holes and tie a bow at the top and bottom. Double-knot the loops.

Add Bows

13 Apply floral adhesive to the back of the invitation. Allow glue to set for a few minutes until it is tacky.

Apply Adhesive

14 Press the invitation firmly into the wreath until it is secure.

Attach Invitation to Wreath

Add Eucalyptus

15 Cut small pieces of eucalyptus. Remove the leaves from the bottom portion of the stems.

16 Insert the stems at an angle randomly throughout the wreath.

Add Caspia

17 Cut small pieces of caspia.

18 Insert the stems at an angle into the wreath as desired. Use floral adhesive on the stems if necessary.

Add Baby's Breath

19 Cut small pieces of baby's breath.

20 Insert the stems into the wreath as desired. Use floral adhesive on the stems to secure them if necessary.

21 Cut small pieces of various colored statice.

22 Insert them at an angle into the wreath as desired.

Add Statice

23 Cut small pieces of German statice.

24 Insert them at an angle into the wreath as desired.

Add German Statice

25 Cut small pieces of various colors of delphinium.

26 Insert them at an angle into the wreath as desired. Because dried delphinium is extremely fragile, use floral adhesive to place it in the wreath.

Add Delphinium

Spray the Wreath

27 Lay the wreath flat on a covered surface indoors or outside.

28 Spray the entire arrangement with clear acrylic gloss to help preserve the flowers, remembering to avoid spraying the ribbon hanger.

Completed Wedding Wreath

MATERIALS

3 yards white 100% cotton muslin

6 yards white-on-white patterned 100% cotton

3 yards off-white 100% cotton

Rotary cutter and mat

Quilter's ruler

3 yards double-sided transfer web paper

Permanent fabric pen

4mm quilter's pins

Iron

White and yellow 40 wt. thread

#7 quilter's needle

15 yards of ½"-wide rose vine appliqué braid

16-gauge clear vinyl plastic (½" bigger on all sides than your wedding invitation)

Masking tape

3 yards lightweight quilt batting

2"-wide wired chiffon ribbon

Glue gun

Three pearl sprays

Wedding invitation

¼"-wide chiffon ribbon

32 1" drop pearls

Quilt a Memory

Cherish each wedding moment with this precious keepsake quilt. At the reception, have guests sign a fabric square with permanent fabric pen. After the wedding, use these signed squares to create a stunning keepsake quilt that will quickly become a beloved heirloom.

NOTE: Before sewing your quilt (see page 3 for Quick Sewing Stitches), follow these guidelines:

- Lay out all of the cut pieces according to the diagram below. That way, you will know if a piece is missing and you can simplify your piecing row by row.

- As you sew each section, put the section back in its original position to make piecing easier (see page 3 for Quick Sewing Stitches).

- Use a ¼" seam allowance when sewing the quilt.

- Prewash all fabric, and press first for easier cutting.

Cutting Directions

• • •

FABRIC	CUTTING QUANTITY	SIZE TO CUT
White patterned cotton	32 background squares	6" x 6" (15cm x 15cm)
Muslin	32 name squares	5" x 5" (13cm x 13cm)
White patterned cotton	1 center square	13½" x 13½" (34cm x 34cm)
Clear vinyl plastic	1 center plastic sleeve	8½" x 6" (22cm x 15cm)
Quilt batting	1 quilt batting	50" x 52" (127cm x 132cm)
White patterned cotton	1 quilt back	50" x 52" (127cm x 132cm)
Off-white cotton	24 bar straps	6" x 2" (15cm x 5cm)
	2 interior bar straps	13½" x 2" (34cm x 5cm)
	2 outside borders	52" x 2" (132cm x 5cm)
	2 top/bottom borders	46" x 2" (117cm x 5cm)
	4 interior sashes	46" x 2" (117cm x 5cm)
	2 short sashes	14" x 2" (36cm x 5cm)

1. Fold the fabric vertically in half with the right sides together. The fold line should follow along the grain of the fabric.

2. Lay the fabric on the cutting mat with the fold line along a grid line. Place the quilter's ruler on the fabric close to the raw edge at a 90° angle to the fold.

3. Use your rotary cutter to trim along the edge of the ruler. Keeping a steady pressure, hold the ruler firmly to keep the fabric from moving. Once the rotary cutter gets past your hand, leave the rotary blade as is and reposition your hand. Hold firmly and continue cutting. Make sure the fabric and ruler do not shift position.

   NOTE: Using double-sided tape, tape three or four thin strips of fine sandpaper at the bottom of your quilter's ruler. This will keep your ruler from slipping while you are cutting.

4. Place the ruler on the fabric, aligning the trimmed edge with the appropriate measurement on the ruler.

5. Hold the ruler firmly and cut as in Step 3. After cutting several strips, check the fabric to make sure all the fabric pieces are "on grain," as in Step 1.

6. Stack several layers of fabric and cut them into crosswise strips rather than cutting each piece of the quilt individually.

7. Once you have cut out all the fabric pieces, lay out all the fabric pieces according to the diagram below. This will show you if something is missing from your quilt pattern.

Cut the Fabric Edges

Cut Out the Fabric Squares

Piece Quilt Together

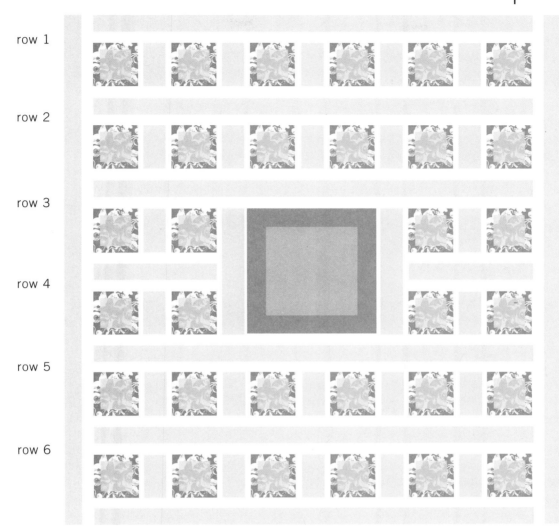

Quilt Layout Diagram

row 1

row 2

row 3

row 4

row 5

row 6

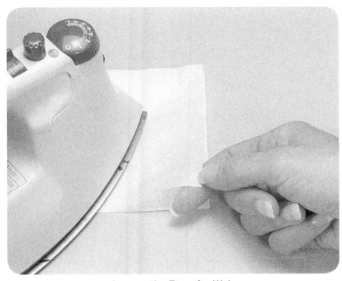

Iron on the Transfer Web

NOTE: The cutting techniques on this page will not only save you time but also keep your cuts more accurate. Before cutting, determine the grain line of the fabric by folding the fabric in half and holding it by the rough edges.

8 Iron the transfer web to the wrong side of all thirty-two white muslin squares by following the directions on the transfer web package.

Continues

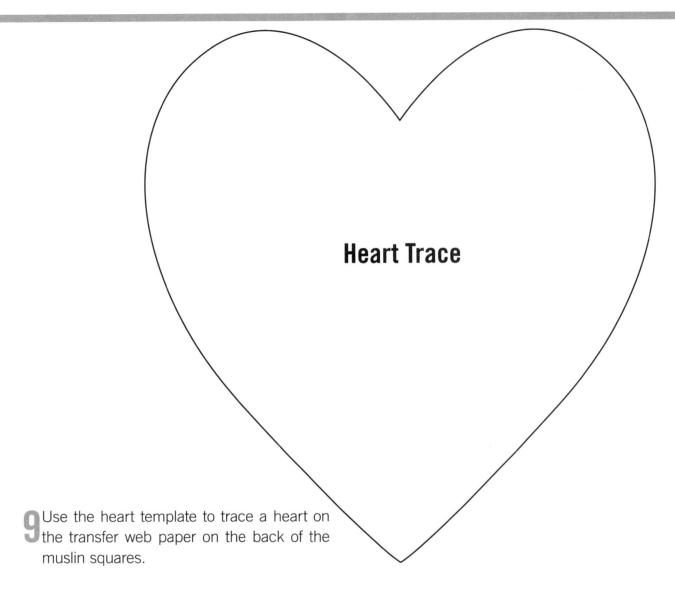

Heart Trace

9 Use the heart template to trace a heart on the transfer web paper on the back of the muslin squares.

10 Cut out all 32 hearts.

11 Use the fabric pen to write names on the right side of the fabric in the center of each heart (or have the guests sign the hearts themselves at the wedding reception to save you a step).

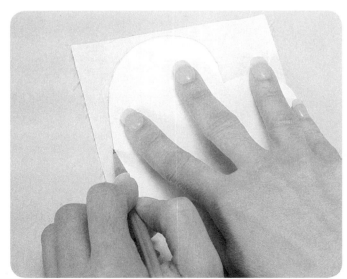

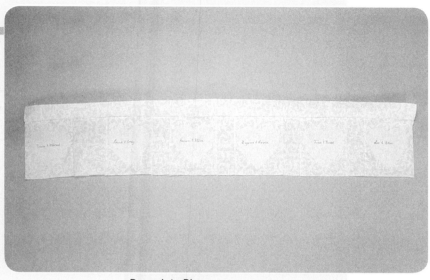

Press into Place

Sew the Squares and Bar Straps Together

12 Score the transfer web paper backing with a pin. Remove all paper from the hearts.

13 Center the hearts on each background fabric square and press into place. (This figure shows rows 1 and 2.)

14 Sew one square at a time (see page 3 for Quick Sewing Stitches), with the right sides of the fabric together, each background square to a 6" × 2" bar strap and return to its proper position.

15 Now sew the opposite side of the background square and a bar strap together. Continue until you complete row 1.

16 Press all seams flat. Repeat this step for rows 2, 3a, 3b, 4a, 4b, 5, and 6 on the quilt-piecing diagram on page 124.

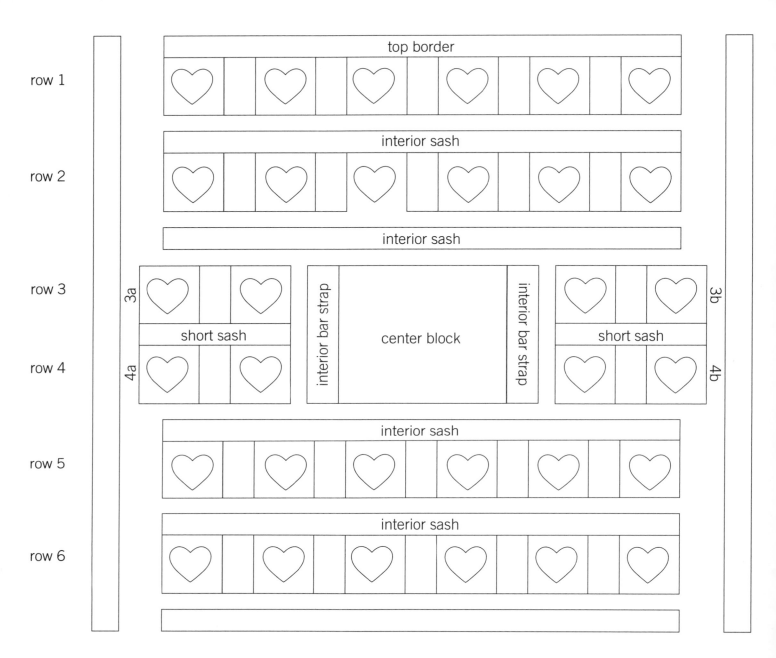

Quilt Diagram

17 With the right sides of the fabric together, sew the top border to row 1, and the interior sashes to rows 2, 5, and 6. Return the rows to their proper layout position as you sew.

18 With the right sides of the fabric together, sew row 3a to a short sash.

19 Sew this unit to row 4a. Repeat for rows 3b and 4b. Sew the two interior bar straps to the center block, one on each side.

20 Sew the three middle blocks together to make one unit and sew the center interior sash to the top. Return all the pieces to their layout position.

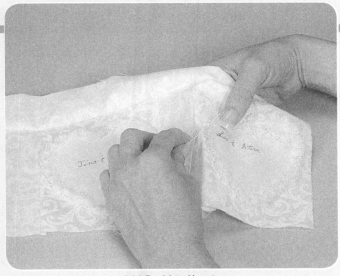

Add Braid to Hearts

21 Pin the rose vine appliqué braid to each heart.

22 Overlap the braid at the top of each heart and trim any excess braid.

23 Hand stitch the braid in place around each heart. See page 3 for Quick Sewing Stitches.

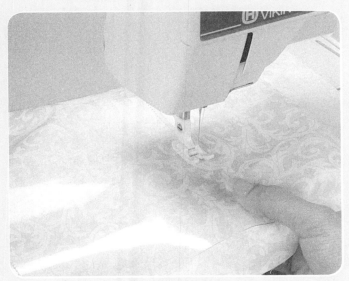

Sew Plastic Pocket

24 Center the clear vinyl plastic on the center square and tape it in place with masking tape (do not use pins).

25 Sew ¼" seam allowance. As you sew the plastic, remove the tape when you come to it to avoid tape adhesive getting on the needle.

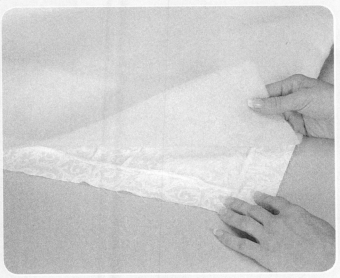

Add Batting

26 Using the diagram on page 126, sew each row together to form the quilt top and press.

27 Place the quilt face-down on the table. Tape all the corners down to keep the quilt from moving around.

28 Lay the batting on top of the quilt, pin it to the quilt, then remove the tape and turn the quilt over.

Continues

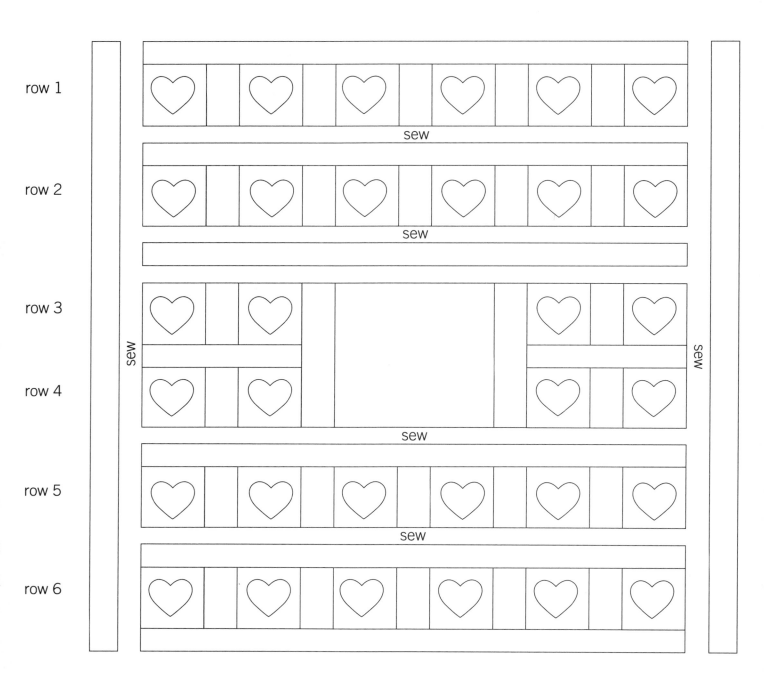

row 1

sew

row 2

sew

row 3

sew

sew

row 4

sew

row 5

sew

row 6

Quilt Diagram

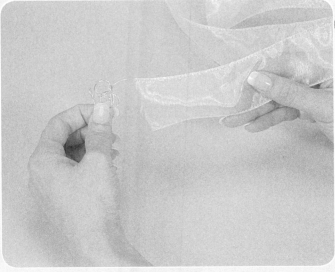

Pulling Out Wire

29 Pull the wire free from one side of the 15 yards of wired chiffon ribbon. When pulling the wire out of the ribbon, wrap the wire into a ball as you pull it out so that the wire keeps under control.

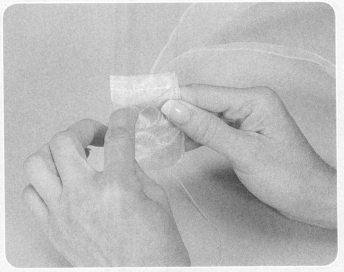

Sew Ribbon Ends

30 Hand stitch the ends of the ribbon together to secure. See page 3 for Quick Sewing Stitches.

31 Cut and tie the thread, making sure the ribbon isn't twisted.

Form Ruffle

32 Pull the wire ends of the chiffon ribbon together and twist. As the ribbon starts to gather, pin the ruffle to the front perimeter of the quilt.

33 Continue to pull the wire, pivoting at the corners and pinning as you continue along the ruffle.

34 Adjust the gathers to fit the quilt front. Do not cut the wire.

Continues

NOTE: The wire side of the ruffle should be next to the edge of the quilt.

35 Hand baste the ribbon ruffle to the quilt and batting ½" from the raw edge. Remove all pins.

36 Pin the quilt back to the front of the quilt over the ruffle with the right sides of the fabric together.

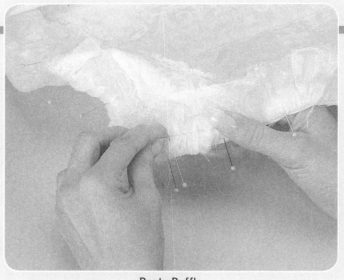

Baste Ruffle

37 Machine stitch around the quilt leaving a 10" opening for turning.

38 Cut the corners diagonally and trim to a ⅛" seam allowance. Untwist the wire ends and remove the rest of the wire from the quilt.

39 Turn the quilt right side out and stitch the opening closed. See page 3 for Quick Sewing Stitches.

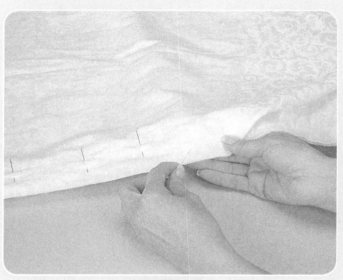

Add Quilt Back

40 Hot glue the rose vine appliqué braid around the clear plastic pocket, leaving the top free.

41 Cut any excess braid and hot glue the ends down.

Add Braid to Pocket

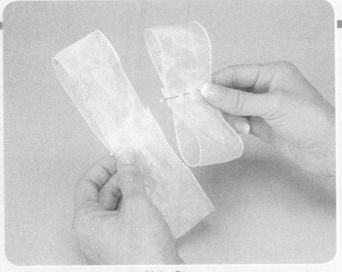

Make Bow

42 Cut two pieces of 2"-wide wired chiffon ribbon to 11½" and 17½". Mark the center of both ribbons.

43 To make the bow, overlap the ribbon ¼" at the center and pin in place.

Sew Bow Together

44 Lay the small bow on top of the large bow, matching the centers. Hand baste both together.

45 Pull the thread to allow the bow to gather in the center. Wrap the thread tightly around the center of the bow a few times.

46 To secure the bow, cut the thread and tie the ends in a knot.

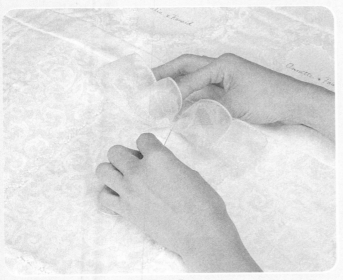

Attach Bow

47 Above the clear plastic pocket, center the bow and hand stitch into place.

Continues

48 On each side of the bow, hot glue two pearl sprays between the small and large loops of the bow.

49 Insert your wedding invitation into the plastic pocket.

50 Hot glue one pearl spray to the center of the bow just under the gather.

> **NOTE:** Try to avoid wearing color nail polish when working with white fabric to avoid stains on the fabric.

51 Cut a 9" length of ¼"-wide chiffon ribbon and mark the center.

52 Hand stitch the ribbon in the center through all three layers of the quilt at every intersection, and tie a triple knot.

53 Tie a shoestring bow with each ribbon.

54 Hot glue a drop pearl to the center of each bow.

> **NOTE:** Feel free to mix it up. This will be a one-of-a-kind quilt where you can showcase your wedding photo instead of your invitation in the center pocket. If you had your dress designed, create the quilt with leftover bridal fabric from your dress.

Add Pearl Spray

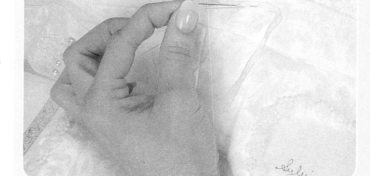

Attach Ribbon

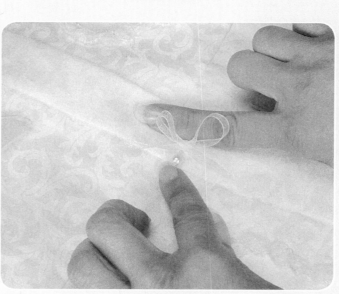

Add Drop Pearl

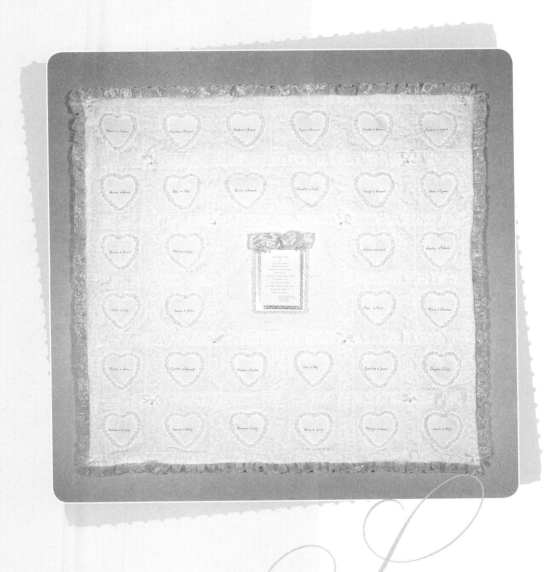

Completed Quilt

2' of ¼"-wide gold ribbon

Floral adhesive

5" × 7" clear acrylic
picture frame

Pipe cleaner or thin stick

Preserved plumosa

Dried delphinium

Dried hydrangea

Picture Perfect

Take any picture frame and personalize it with decorative ribbon,
dried flowers, and any other item that makes it feel worthy as part
of your wedding keepsakes collection. Simple to create, this picture
frame makes a gift for the wedding couple or a thoughtful gift for
family and friends.

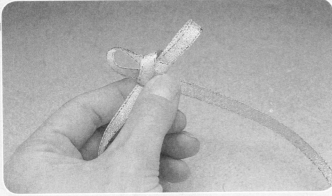

Tie Ribbon

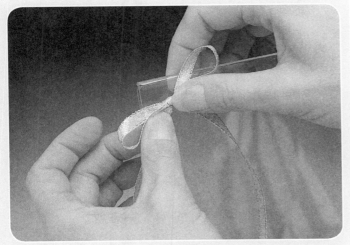

Attach Bow

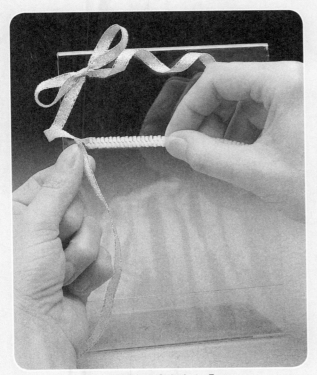

Attach Ribbon Spirals to Frame

1 Tie a shoestring bow in the middle of the ribbon, being sure to keep the loops small.

2 Pull the loops tight to knot the center.

3 Place a small dot-sized amount of floral adhesive on the back of the knot.

4 Firmly press the ribbon to the frame at an angle in the upper left-hand corner.

5 Twist the ribbon ends to create spirals. One end of the ribbon will spiral across the top of the frame, while the other will spiral down the left side of the frame.

6 Apply floral adhesive to the back of the first twist of ribbon where it will make contact with the frame and press it into place.

7 Use a pipe cleaner or another thin stick to help apply the glue and attach the ribbon spirals to the frame.

8 Continue twisting and attaching loops until it's no longer possible.

9 Trim the ribbon with a diagonal cut.

Continues

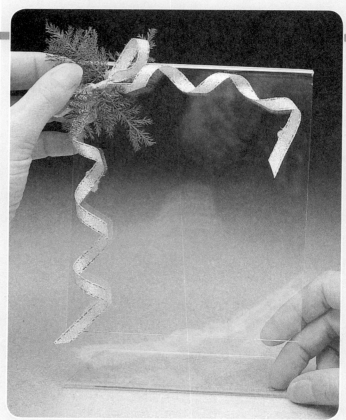

Add Greenery

10 Trim pieces of plumosa. Glue the tips of the stems around the center of the bow.

11 Cut individual delphinium blossoms from the stalk.

> **NOTE:** Handle the dried flowers carefully to avoid crumbling them.

12 Place a small amount of glue on the back of each blossom and attach them where the ribbon loops touch the frame.

13 Cut a few unopened buds of the delphinium along with the stems to use around the center of the bow.

Add Delphinium

Add Hydrangea

14 Cut individual hydrangea blossoms.

15 Place a small amount of glue on the back of each blossom and place them along the ribbon as desired.

Completed
Picture Perfect

MATERIALS

Spiral-bound memory book,
photo album, scrapbook,
or guest book
(a 9½" x 8½" memory album
is used here)

½ yard of decorative moiré
fabric depending on book size
(1 yard of 54"-wide moiré was
used for this memory album)

Poster board

Fabric glue

1 yard of quilt batting

⅞"-wide grosgrain ribbon
(2 yards was used for this
memory album)

1 stem silk dogwood
(or silk flower of your choice)

Floral adhesive

⅝"-wide sheer ribbon

Memories Album

Embellish a photo album, journal, scrap-, or guestbook by using pastel-colored, shimmery fabric, ribbons, and silk blossoms to create a special directory to your big day. Perfect for saving all engagement and wedding mementos, cherished photographs, guest wishes, as well as any other senti-mental moment you'll want to remember for a long time to come.

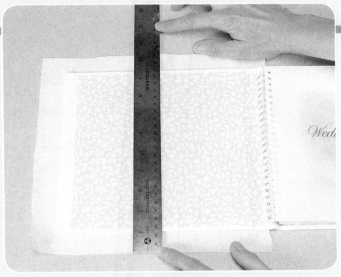

Measure Cover Fabric

1 Measure the height and width of the book cover. (The fabric should come within ¼" of the spirals and add 1" fabric to all sides.)

2 Cut two pieces of fabric to size, one for the front cover and one for the back.

NOTE: If using a fabric with a pattern or grain, make sure the fabric matches on both front and back pieces.

Reinforce Edge

3 Cut two 1"-wide strips of poster board the same height as the book cover.

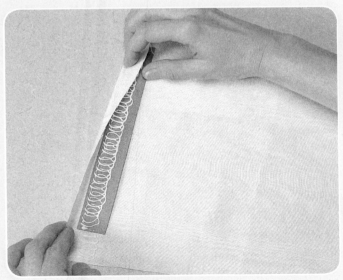

Glue Edge

4 Turn the fabric face down, making sure your pattern or grain runs from top to bottom.

5 Place the poster board strip ½" from the edge of the fabric, making sure the strip is evenly spaced between the top and bottom of the fabric.

6 Apply fabric glue to the back of the poster board strip. Fold the ½" edge of fabric onto the strip and glue firmly into place.

Continues ➤

7 Unfold the glued poster board strip so the fabric lies flat with the wrong side face up.

8 Cut a piece of quilt batting that is ½" shorter on three sides than the side with the batting up against the inside edge of the poster board strip.

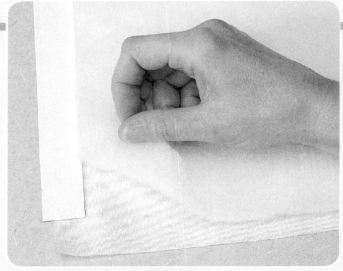

Insert Quilt Batting

9 Fold the poster board strip over onto the fabric, sandwiching the batting between the strip and the fabric.

10 Apply fabric glue along the strip.

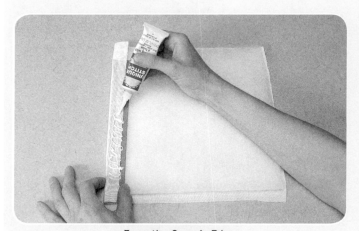

Form the Cover's Edge

11 Carefully glue the edged fabric to the cover of the album.

NOTE: The edge with the poster board strip should lie next to the spiral binding on both the front and back. Place a heavy weight on it until the glue is firmly set.

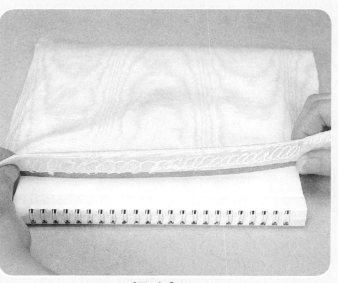

Attach Cover

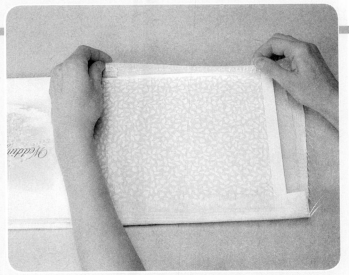

Finish Top and Bottom Edges

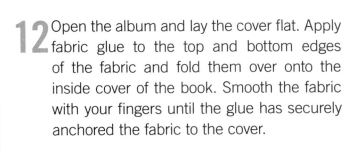

12 Open the album and lay the cover flat. Apply fabric glue to the top and bottom edges of the fabric and fold them over onto the inside cover of the book. Smooth the fabric with your fingers until the glue has securely anchored the fabric to the cover.

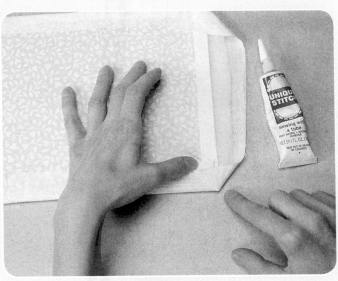

Fold Corners

13 Fold the corners as shown in the figure to create finished edges. Apply fabric glue under the folds to secure the fabric.

Finish Outer Edge

14 Apply fabric glue to the outside edge of the fabric and fold it over onto the cover. Make sure the corners are tightly folded. Smooth the fabric with your fingers until the glue has securely anchored the fabric to the cover.

Continues

15 Cut a piece of poster board slightly smaller than the inside cover.

Cut Inside Cover Board

16 Cut a piece of fabric large enough that each side overlaps the poster board by 1". Make sure to properly position any fabric pattern or grain.

17 Apply fabric glue to the edges of the fabric and fold them over onto the back side of the poster board using the same technique as in Steps 12–14.

NOTE: Do not glue the fabric to the front of the poster board.

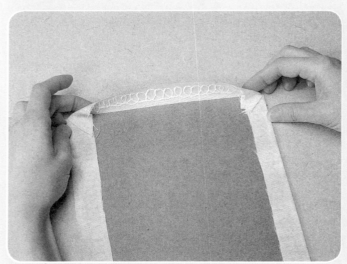

Glue Fabric to Board

18 Apply fabric glue to the back side of the poster board and glue it into place on the inside book cover. Place a heavy weight on it until the glue has adhered completely.

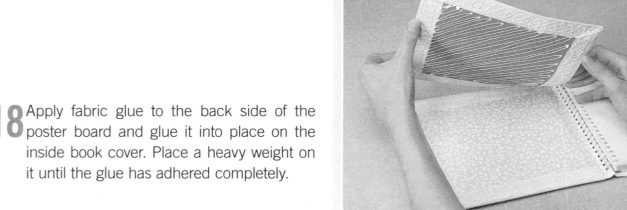

Glue Board to Inside Cover

Complete Inside Covers

19 Repeat Steps 16–18 for the back cover.

> **NOTE:** Make sure to properly position any fabric pattern or grain.

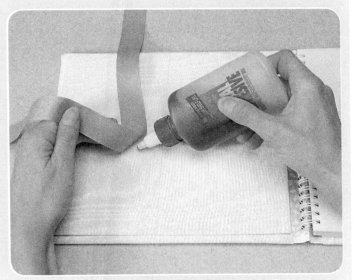

Wrap Ribbon Around Cover

20 Wrap a piece of grosgrain ribbon lengthwise around the front cover (length will vary according to book size) and cut it so the ends overlap by 1". Offset the ribbon slightly to the outside of the guest book.

21 On the inside front cover, place a small amount of floral adhesive on the center of the ribbon to secure it.

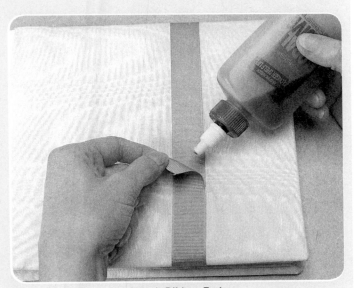

Attach Ribbon Ends

22 Bring the ribbon ends around to the front of the book cover and glue them in place using a small amount of floral adhesive.

> **NOTE:** Make sure the ends overlap at the point where the bow will be placed.

Continues

23 Cut a 28" length of grosgrain ribbon.

24 Glue the center of the ribbon to the cover with floral adhesive. When the adhesive has set securely, tie a shoestring bow, making the loops 1" longer than the desired final length.

Add Bow

25 Cut two dogwood blossoms leaving 2" of stem. Try to find flowers with leaves close to them if possible.

26 Lay the stems opposite each other over the center of the bow.

Add Flowers

27 Double-knot the shoestring bow around the flower stems.

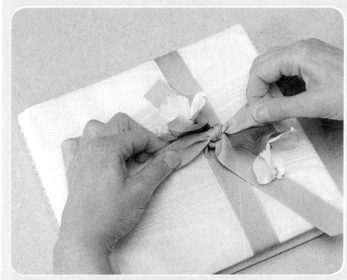

Secure Flowers

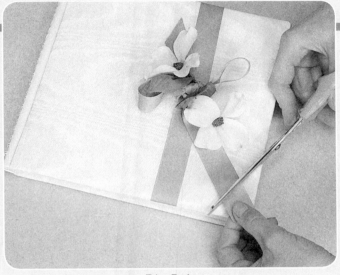

Trim Ends

28 Adjust the flowers and bow loops as desired. Trim the ribbon ends with diagonal cuts.

29 Place a small amount of floral adhesive on the ends of the ribbons and ribbon loops, allowing the glue to set for a few minutes until it gets tacky.

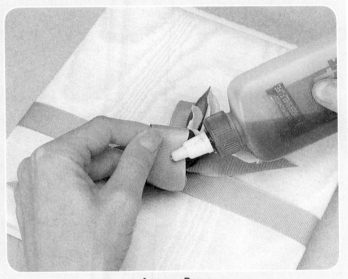

Arrange Bow

30 Gently press the ribbon ends and loops into place on the cover.

NOTE: Place only a small amount of glue on the ribbons so as to make sure the glue will not bleed through.

Add Flowers

31 If desired, surround the bow with more dogwood blossoms. Glue one or two petals of each blossom to the cover to hold it in place.

Continues

32 Leaving the sheer ribbon on the roll, thread the ribbon inside the spiral binding to use as a bookmark. A letter opener or tweezers may be useful to help thread the ribbon. The ribbon extending out of the bottom of the spirals should be trimmed to approximately 6". Trim the other end to approximately twice the height of the book.

NOTE: It is helpful to open the album to relieve pressure on the spirals.

33 Cut several 18" lengths of sheer ribbon.

NOTE: The number of bows needed will depend on the size of your album and the number of spirals you decide to wrap with a bow. For this example, every two spirals was wrapped with a bow. Count the spirals ahead of time and plan how many you will wrap.

34 Thread the ribbon under the spirals and center it. Tie shoestring bows, lining up the loops to a little longer than the desired finished size.

35 Double-knot the loops and trim the ribbon ends with diagonal cuts as you move down the spine.

36 Tie a loose knot in the ribbon that extends through the bottom of the spirals to prevent the ribbon from sliding out. If the spirals are large, make a knot or bow to anchor the ribbon.

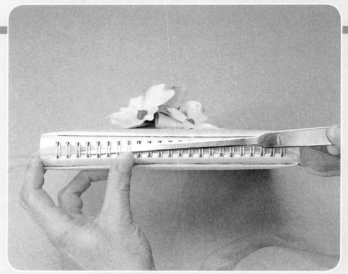

Thread Ribbon Through Spiral

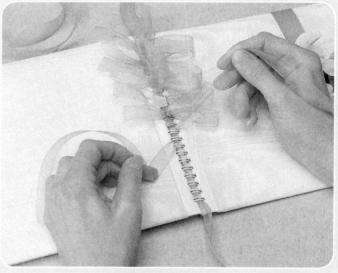

Add Bows to Spine

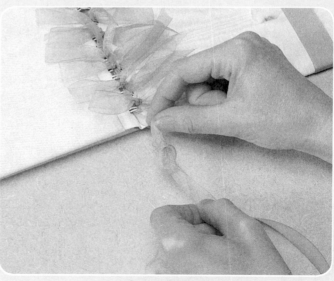

Anchor Ribbon

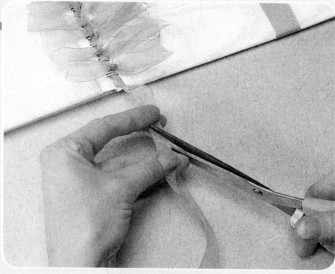

Finish Ribbon End

Finish Bookmark

37 Pull the ribbon up through the spirals until the knot is at the base of the spirals.

38 Trim the end of the ribbon with a V-cut.

39 Open the album and bring the other end of the bookmark ribbon down over the center of the book.

40 Attach a single dogwood blossom with floral adhesive below where the bookmark extends beyond the pages.

41 Trim the end of the ribbon with a V-cut 3" below the blossom.

Completed Memories Album

Resources

Botanique Preservation Equipment, Inc.
16601 N 25th Ave
Suite 101
Phoenix, AZ 85023
www.botaniquefrzdry.com

C.M. Offray & Son, Inc.
360 Route 24
Chester, NJ 07930
800-551-LION
www.offray.com

Coats & Clark, Inc.
30 Patewood Drive
Suite #351
Greenville, SC 29615
864-281-5521
www.coatsandclark.com

Design Master Color Tool Inc.
P.O. Box 601
Boulder, CO 80306
303-443-5214
www.dmcolor.com

Fiskars, Inc.
305 84th Ave. South
Wausau, WI 54401
715-842-2091
www.fiskars.com

Florist Directory
www.eflorist.com

Home-Sew
P.O. Box 4099
Bethlehem, PA 18018
800-344-4739

John Henry Company
5800 Grand River Ave.
P.O. Box 17099
Lansing, MI 48901
800-748-0517
www.jhc.com

Knud Nielson Company, Inc.
P.O. Box 746
Evergreen, AL 36401

Mariemont Florist, Inc.
7257 Wooster Pike
Cincinnati, OH 45227
800-437-3567
www.mariemontflorist.com

Mountain Mist
100 Williams Street
Cincinnati, OH 45215
800-345-7150
www.stearnstextiles.com

Oasis Floral Products
P.O. Box 118
Kent, OH 44240
800-321-8286

Pokon Chrysal
3036 N.W. 107th Ave.
Miami, FL 33172
800-247-9725
www.pokonchrysalusa.com

Society of American Florists
1601 Duke St.
Alexandria, VA 22314
800-336-4743
www.safnow.org

Them O Web
770 Glenn Ave.
Wheeling, IL 60090
www.themoweb.com

VABAN Ribbon
165 Eighth St.
San Francisco, CA 94103
800-448-9988

W.J. Cowee, Inc.
28 Taylor Ave.
P.O. Box 248
Berlin, NY 12022
800-658-2233
www.cowee.com

Wrights
85 South Street
West Warren, MA 01092
www.wrights.com

www.blisswedding.com
www.bridalguide.com
www.bridesofcolor.com
www.TheKnot.com
www.ModernBride.com
www.usabride.com
www.weddingbells.com

Acknowledgments

A very special thanks to all of the contributors in this publication, specifically:

Jacquelynne Johnson for the following projects:

The Bride's Veil, page 66
Ring Cushion, page 78
Elegant Bridal Wrap, page 86
Quilt a Memory, page 118

Terry L. Rye for the following projects:

Floral Frosting, page 23
Ivy Pew Décor, page 34
Floral Garland, page 46
The Flower Girl's Pomander, page 74
Sweetheart Hair Comb, page 84
Unity Candle, page 100

Terry L. Rye and **Laurel Tudor** for the following projects:

Origami Place Settings, page 16
Statuesque Centerpiece, page 27
Wedding Wishes Card Cage, page 39
Mini Bouquet Napkin Ring, page 52
Bride and Groom Thrones, page 57
Satin Tote, page 92
Bow Bouquet, page 106
Wedding Wreath, page 111
Picture Perfect, page 132
Memories Album, page 136

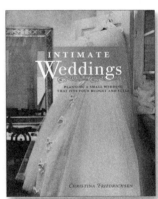

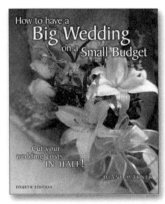

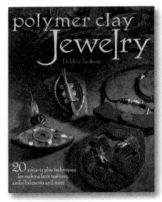
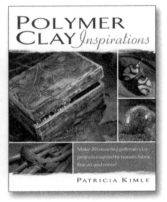

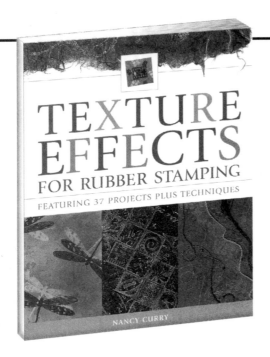

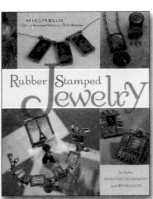